North Carolina State Building Code:
Administrative Code and Policies

2012

North Carolina State Building Code: Administrative Code and Policies, 2012 edition

First Printing: January 2012
Second Printing: August 2012
Third Printing: November 2013

ISBN-978-1-60983-123-3

COPYRIGHT © 2011
by
INTERNATIONAL CODE COUNCIL, INC.

T020762

PREFACE of the 2012 NORTH CAROLINA STATE BUILDING CODES

North Carolina has been a pioneer in the field of Statewide Building Regulations that have been enacted for the protection of the public. The Building Laws passed in 1903 and 1905 created a Building Code for materials and methods of construction in use at that time in the State.

The General Assembly of 1933 created a Building Code Council and authorized it to, in cooperation with the Commissioner of Insurance, prepare and adopt a State Building Code. The first State Building Code was adopted in 1935 and ratified by the 1941 General Assembly.

The 1957 Legislature rewrote the 1933 Act, ratified the 1953 Edition, and reorganized and expanded the membership and responsibility of the Council. The 1953 Edition of the State Building Code was revised in accordance with the 1957 Act and printed as the 1958 Edition.

The 1933 Act of the General Assembly provided that any city or county could adopt any building regulation that was more stringent than the State Building Code regulations. However, after a General Assembly Study Commission Report, the 1957 Legislature provided that any local building regulation that was different from the State regulation would have to be approved by the Building Code Council. The Council adopted a policy to only approve local amendments to the State Code that were absolutely necessary. The policy includes that when the Council sees the need for local amendments, they would be incorporated as a part of the State Building Code in lieu of approving the regulations applying to a specific city or county unless local conditions warranted such specific regulations.

The 1967 Edition of the State Building Code was prepared utilizing the framework of the *Standard Building Code*, with several chapters taken from the American Insurance Association's *National Building Code* and the egress chapter taken from the *Life Safety Code* of NFPA.

The 1978, 1991 and 1996 Editions were prepared by the Building Code Council with the assistance of specially appointed Advisory and Ad-Hoc Committees representing Code Enforcement Officials, Contractors, Designers and others affected by the regulations. These Editions were the latest *Standard Building Code* with North Carolina amendments.

The 2002, 2006, 2009 and 2012 Editions were prepared by Ad-Hoc Committees representing Code Enforcement Officials, Contractors, Designers and others affected by the regulations. These Editions were the *International Building Code* with North Carolina amendments.

The 2012 North Carolina State Code is presented with the hope that its use will protect the public from dangerous and unsanitary buildings. This Code is intended to provide Code Enforcement Officials, Contractors and Designers a set of minimum standards to follow in design and construction. The Building Code Council has the authority to amend the Code when the wider use of materials and methods comply with the safety standards set forth in the laws.

PREFACE of the 2012 NORTH CAROLINA ADMINISTRATIVE CODE and POLICIES

The purpose of the *North Carolina Administrative Code and Policies* is to serve as a comprehensive document to guide decisions aimed at protecting the public's health, safety and welfare in the built environment. This protection is provided through the enforcement, by state and local governments, of the technical codes incorporated by reference herein.

The *North Carolina Administrative Code* was first adopted by the Building Council in 1991. The 1996 and 2002 Editions were published in conjunction with the subsequent Code Editions. The 2006 *North Carolina Administrative Code and Policies* was a reorganization and rewrite of the 2002 *Administration and Enforcements Code*. The 2009 and 2012 Edition of the *North Carolina Administrative Code and Policies* is an administrative update of the 2006 *Administration and Enforcements Code*. Chapter 1, Administrative Code, contains Rules adopted by the Building Code Council and approved by the Rules Review Commission. Chapter 2, Policies, contains generally accepted policies and procedures based on the North Carolina General Statutes. Chapter 3, Referenced Statutes, contains references to many applicable General Statutes. The appendices include representative administrative forms.

EDITIONS of the NORTH CAROLINA STATE BUILDING CODES

Administrative	1991, 1996, 2002, 2006, 2009, 2012
Building	1936, 1953, 1958, 1967, 1978, 1991, 1996, 2002, 2006, 2009, 2012
Residential	1968, 1993, 1997, 2002, 2006, 2009, 2012
Accessibility	1973, 1991, 1999

(Accessibility requirements were part of the Building Code before 9/1/1973 and after 1/1/2009.)

Electrical (NEC)	1931, 1933, 1935, 1937, 1940, 1942, 1943, 1947, 1949, 1951, 1953, 1954, 1955, 1956, 1957, 1958, 1959, 1962, 1965, 1968, 1971, 1975, 1978, 1981, 1984, 1987, 1990, 1993, 1996, 1999, 2002, 2005, 2008, 2011
Fire	1991, 1996, 2002, 2006, 2009, 2012
Mechanical	1971, 1980, 1991, 1996, 2002, 2006, 2009, 2012
Energy Conservation	1991, 1996, 2002, 2006, 2009, 2012
Plumbing	1963, 1968, 1980, 1991, 1996, 2002, 2006, 2009, 2012
Fuel Gas	1991, 1996, 2002, 2006, 2009, 2012

ACKNOWLEDGEMENTS
2012 North Carolina Ad Hoc Committees

2012 NC-IBC 2009
Building Chapters 1-15, 34-end

Butch Simmons, NCBCC, Chair
Rick Ball, Architect
Barry Gupton, NCDOI
John Hitch, NCBCC
Lon McSwain, Mecklenburg County
David Lindsay, Greensboro
Alan Perdue, NCBCC
Charles Theisen, Arcvision
Tom Yount, Integrated Design

2012 NC-IBC 2009
Building Chapters 16-33

Steve Knight, NCBCC, Chair
Mark Bailey, NCDOI
Mike Huslage, Bobbitt
Paul Lavene, CCMA
Bill Murchinson, Engineer
Dan Murray, NCBCC
Frank Park, Guilford County
Bob Ruffner, NCBCC
Dennis Williams, Williams Design

2012 NC-IECC 2009
Energy Conservation

Tom Turner, NCBCC, Chair
Al Bass, NCBCC
Doug Brinkley, PBCL
Chad Chandler, Architect
Reid Conway, State Energy Office
Billy Hinton, NCDOI
Renee Hutcheson, Small Kane
Dennis Maidon, Wake County
Margie Mears, Mathis
Robert Privott, NCHBA
John Roberts, IES Engineers
Kim Reitterer, NCBCC
Janie Sutton, NCDOI

Jeff Tiller, Appalachian State University
Hawley Truax, NCBCC
John Wiggins, UL

2012 NC-IFC 2009
Fire

Alan Perdue, NCBCC, Chair
Mike Edwards, Edwards Electronics
Dana Graham, J and D Sprinkler
Wayne Hamilton, Asheville
Steve Hensley, Associated Sprinkler
Charlie Johnson, Wake County
Derrick Johnson, Electrical and Fire Alarm
Jeff Johnson, Consultant
Chuck Kimball, Brooks Equipment
Bryan Moffitt, CJMW
Robbie Pate, Rocky Mount
Richard Strickland, NCDOI
John Wiggins, UL

2012 NC-IFGC 2009
Fuel Gas

Ralph Euchner, NCBCC, Chair
Steve Abernathy, Piedmont Natural Gas
Mike Boggs, NC Propane Gas Association
Larry Currin, Public Service NC
Don Ferguson, Piedmont Natural Gas
Mike Gibson, Fayetteville
Skip Higgins, Contractor
Billy Hinton, NCDOI
Marshall Perry, Greensboro
Paula Strickland, NCBCC
Henry Webster, NCDOI
John Wiggins, UL

2012 NC-IMC 2009
Mechanical

Al Bass, NCBCC, Chair

Alec Arthur, Asheville

Mike Gibson, Fayetteville

Skip Higgins, Contractor

Billy Hinton, NCDOI

Paula Strickland, NCBCC

Mike Norris, Winston-Salem

Lacy Smith, Guilford County

Janie Sutton, NCDOI

Henry Webster, NCDOI

2012 NC-IPC 2009
Plumbing

Al Bass, NCBCC, Chair

Wallace Cole, Winston-Salem

Dale Dawson, PHFS Board

Donny Denny, Contractor

Phil Edwards, Mecklenburg County

Billy Hinton, NCDOI

Ken Keplar, Wake County

Jim Lawson, High Point

Bill McElrath, Reece, Roland & McElrath

Tommy Poole, American Plumbing

Paula Strickland, NCBCC

Henry Webster, NCDOI

2012 NC-IRC 2009
Residential

David Smith, NCBCC, Chair

David Conner, NCDOI

Jeff Griffin, Mecklenburg County

Steve Knight, NCBCC

Jim Lane, Raleigh

Mike Page, NCDOI

Robert Privott, NCHBA

Leon Skinner, Raleigh

Dan Tingen, NCBCC

Hawley Truax, NCBCC

Tom Turner, NCBCC

Hiram Williams, Action Construction

NORTH CAROLINA STATE BUILDING CODE COUNCIL
OCTOBER 1, 2013
www.ncbuildingcodes.com

Al Bass, Jr., PE – 15
(Mechanical Engineer)
Bass, Nixon and Kennedy
6425 Chapman Court
Raleigh, NC 27612
919-782-4689

Dan Tingen – 17
(Home Builder)
Tingen Construction Co.
8411 Garvey Drive, #101
Raleigh, NC 27616
919-875-2161

John Hitch, AIA – 16
(Architect)
Smith Sinnett Arch.
4600 Lake Boone Tr., Ste. 205
Raleigh, NC 27607
919-781-8582

Janice Cox – 13
(Electrical Contractor)
Fruitt Electric
PO Box 7
Randleman, NC 27317
336-370-9924

Lon McSwain – 15
(Building Inspector)
Mecklenburg County
700 North Tryon Street
Charlotte, NC 28202
704-336-4302

Kim Reitterer, PE – 13
(Electrical Engineer)
ELM Engineering
900 Center Park Dr., Ste. E
Charlotte, NC 28217
704-335-0396

Ralph Euchner – 19
(Gas Industry)
PSNC Energy
PO Box 1398
Gastonia, NC 28053
704-810-3331

Mack Nixon – 16
(County Representative)
Albemarle Home Builders
199 Mill Street
Elizabeth City, NC 27909
252-338-5211

Bob Ruffner, Jr. – 15
(General Contractor)
Clancy and Theys Construction
PO Box 4189
Wilmington, NC 28406
910-392-5220

Leah Faile, AIA – 16
(Architect)
O'Brien/Atkins Assoc., PA
PO Box 12037
RTP, NC 27709
919-941-9000

Mack Paul – 17
(Public Representative)
Morningstar Law Group
630 Davis Drive, Ste. 300
Morrisville, NC 27560
919-590-0377

David Smith – 16
(Coastal Contractor)
D. Smith Builder
905 Saltwood Lane
Wilmington, NC 28411
910-681-0394

Steve Knight, PE – 15
(Structural Engineer)
Steve L. Knight, PE
1507 Mount Vernon Ave.
Statesville, NC 28677
704-878-2996

Alan Perdue – 15
(Fire Services)
Guilford County
1002 Meadowood Street
Greensboro, NC 27409
336-641-7565

Scott Stevens – 16
(Municipal Representative)
City Manager
PO Drawer A
Goldsboro, NC 27533
919-580-4330

Cindy Register, PE – 17
(State Agency)
State Construction
301 North Wilmington St.
Raleigh, NC 27601
919-807-4127

Paula Strickland – 19
(Mechanical Contractor)
Williams PH&AC
1051 Grecade Street
Greensboro, NC 27408
336-275-1328

NORTH CAROLINA
DEPARTMENT OF INSURANCE

www.ncdoi.com/osfm
919-661-5880

By Statute, the Commissioner of Insurance has general supervision of the administration and enforcement of the North Carolina State Building Code, and the Engineering Division serves as the Staff for the Building Code Council. Officials of the Department of Insurance are:

WAYNE GOODWIN
Commissioner

RICK McINTYRE
Senior Deputy Commissioner

CHRIS NOLES, PE
Deputy Commissioner

BARRY GUPTON, PE
Chief Code Consultant

MIKE PAGE, PE
Administrative Code Consultant

COMMITTEES OF THE COUNCIL
OCTOBER 1, 2013

ADMINISTRATION
Dan Tingen – Chair
John Hitch, AIA – Vice Chair
Al Bass, PE
Ralph Euchner
John Hitch, AIA
Steve Knight, PE
Lon McSwain
Alan Perdue
Kim Reitterer, PE
David Smith

BUILDING
Lon McSwain – Chair
Janice Cox
Leah Faile, AIA
John Hitch, AIA
Alan Perdue
Cindy Register, PE
Bob Ruffner, Jr.
Paula Strickland

ELECTRICAL
Kim Reitterer, PE – Chair
Al Bass, PE
Janice Cox
Leah Faile, AIA
John Hitch, AIA
Cindy Register, PE
Bob Ruffner, Jr.

ENERGY
Ralph Euchner – Chair
Al Bass, PE
Mack Nixon
Mack Paul
Kim Reitterer, PE
Bob Ruffner, Jr.
David Smith
Scott Stevens

FIRE PREVENTION
Alan Perdue – Chair
Ralph Euchner
John Hitch, AIA
Mack Nixon
Mack Paul
Bob Ruffner, Jr.

MECHANICAL
Al Bass, PE – Chair
Janice Cox
Ralph Euchner
David Smith
Paula Strickland

RESIDENTIAL
David Smith – Chair
Ralph Euchner
Steve Knight, PE
Lon McSwain
Mack Nixon
Cindy Register, PE
Paula Strickland

STRUCTURAL
Steve Knight, PE – Chair
Al Bass, PE
Leah Faile, AIA
John Hitch, AIA
Bob Ruffner, Jr.
Scott Stevens

TABLE OF CONTENTS

CHAPTER 1

ADMINISTRATIVE CODE

SECTION 101
TITLE AND SCOPE

101.1 Title. This document is "The North Carolina Administrative Code and Policies," hereinafter known as "this code." Any references to International Codes shall refer to North Carolina State Building Codes.

101.2 Purpose. The purpose of this code is to provide for the administration and enforcement of the North Carolina State Building Codes as adopted by the Building Code Council and enforced by State and local code enforcement officials. This code is incorporated by reference into the North Carolina Building, Accessibility, Plumbing, Mechanical, Electrical, Fire Prevention, Fuel Gas, Energy Conservation, Existing Buildings, Rehabilitation, and Residential Codes, hereinafter referred to collectively as the "technical codes." This code is intended to provide for the administrative aspects of each of the technical codes. In this code, the plumbing, mechanical, electrical, fire prevention and gas systems shall be referred to as "service systems."

101.3 Scope.

101.3.1 Requirements of other state agencies, occupational licensing boards or commissions. The North Carolina State Building Codes do not include all additional requirements for buildings and structures that may be imposed by other state agencies, occupational licensing boards or commissions. It shall be the responsibility of a permit holder, design professional, contractor or occupational license holder to determine whether any additional requirements exist.

> *Commentary: Many State agencies, occupational licensing boards or commissions have specific design and construction requirements that are not incorporated into the North Carolina State Building Codes and are not enforced by code enforcement officials. Permit holders, design professionals, contractors or occupational license holders should consult with any relevant boards or agencies to determine whether there are any additional construction and design requirements for their projects.*

101.3.2 Technical Codes.

101.3.2.1 North Carolina Building Code. The provisions of the Building Code shall apply to the construction, alteration, repair, equipment, use and occupancy, location, movement to another site, removal and demolition, or any appurtenances connected or attached to every building or structure, other than one- or two-family dwellings and townhouses.

101.3.2.2 North Carolina Accessibility Provisions. The accessibility provisions shall apply to the construction, alteration, repair, replacement, equipment, appliances, fixtures, fittings and appurtenances of all buildings or structures, other than one- and two-family dwellings and townhouses.

101.3.2.3 North Carolina Plumbing Code. The provisions of the Plumbing Code shall apply to every plumbing installation, including alterations, repairs, replacement, equipment, appliances, fixtures, fittings and appurtenances.

101.3.2.4 North Carolina Mechanical Code. The provisions of the Mechanical Code shall apply to the installation of mechanical systems, including alterations, repairs, replacement, equipment, appliances, fixtures, fittings and appurtenances, including ventilating, heating, cooling, air-conditioning and refrigeration systems, incinerators and other energy-related systems.

101.3.2.5 North Carolina Electrical Code. The provisions of the Electrical Code shall apply to the installation of electrical systems, including alterations, repairs, replacement, equipment, appliances, fixtures, fittings and appurtenances.

101.3.2.6 North Carolina Fire Prevention Code. The provisions of the Fire Prevention Code shall apply to the repair, equipment, use, occupancy and maintenance of every existing building or structure, other than one- or two-family dwellings and townhouses. The provisions of the fire prevention code shall apply to the installation of fire protection systems.

101.3.2.7 North Carolina Fuel Gas Code. The provisions of the Fuel Gas Code shall apply to the installation of gas piping systems extending from the point of delivery to the inlet connections of equipment served, and the installation and operation of residential and commercial gas appliances and related accessories.

101.3.2.8 North Carolina Energy Conservation Code. The provisions of the Energy Conservation Code shall apply to the thermal envelope of the building and installation of energy systems, including alterations, repairs, replacement, equipment, appliances, fixtures, fittings and appurtenances, ventilating, heating, cooling, air-conditioning and refrigeration systems, incinerators and other energy-related systems.

101.3.2.9 North Carolina Existing Buildings Code. All work on any building that undergoes alterations, repairs, replacement, rehabilitation or change of occupancy shall comply with the Existing Buildings Code or the technical codes for the proposed work.

101.3.2.10 North Carolina Rehabilitation Code. All work on any building that undergoes alterations, repairs, replacement, rehabilitation or change of occupancy shall comply with the Rehabilitation Code or the technical codes for the proposed work.

101.3.2.11 North Carolina Residential Code. The provisions of the Residential Code shall apply to the construction, alteration, movement, enlargement, replacement, repair, equipment, use and occupancy, location, removal and demolition of detached one- and two-family dwellings and multiple single-family dwellings (townhouses) not more than three stories in height with a separate means of egress and their accessory structures.

Commentary: Exceptions to the technical codes. Note that there are statutory exceptions to the applicability of the technical codes. These exceptions can be found in North Carolina General Statutes (NCGS) § 143-138(b). The exceptions include (1) farm buildings located outside the jurisdiction of any municipality; (2) equipment for storing, handling, transporting and utilizing liquefied petroleum gases for fuel purposes and (3) equipment or facilities, other than buildings, of a public utility, as defined in NCGS § 62-3, or of an electric or telephone membership corporation, including poles, towers and other structures supporting electric or communication lines.

Commentary: Farm building means any building that is not open to the general public and is used primarily for a bona fide farm purpose. A bona fide farm purpose includes the production or storage of agricultural products or commodities, including crops, fruits, vegetables, ornamental or flowering plants, dairy, timber, livestock, poultry and all other forms of agricultural products. Farm buildings do not include such buildings used for purposes of education and research.

101.3.3 Workmanship. Workmanship is not within the purview of the technical codes unless specifically stated within the code.

101.3.4 Appendices. Provisions in the appendices shall not be enforceable unless specifically incorporated in the technical codes.

Commentary: Use of appendices. An appendix is part of the technical codes only when the technical code specifically references that appendix in the body of the technical code. Conversely, appendices that are not referenced in the technical codes are not part of the North Carolina Building Codes. These nonenforceable appendices are provided solely for the convenience of the reader. Each appendix will indicate under its title whether it is enforceable and required as part of the technical code.

101.3.5 Referenced standards. Standards referenced in the technical codes shall be considered an integral part of the codes. If specific portions of a standard are denoted by code text, only those specific portions of the standard shall be enforced. Where code provisions conflict with a standard, the code provisions shall be enforced. Permissive and advisory provisions in a standard shall not be construed as mandatory.

101.3.6 Existing buildings. Additions, alterations, repairs, replacement, rehabilitations or changes of occupancy shall be permitted to any existing structure or service system without requiring the existing systems to comply with all the requirements of the current building codes. All new work shall conform to the requirements of the technical codes for new construction except as modified by either the existing buildings code or the rehabilitation code. For any portion of an existing building or service system that creates a hazard or unsafe condition, the code enforcement official shall determine the extent to which that portion of the existing building or service system is to be upgraded to conform to the requirements of either the Existing Buildings Code, the Rehabilitation Code or the technical codes.

SECTION 102
RULE-MAKING TO AMEND THE TECHNICAL CODES

102.1 Petition for rule-making.

1. Any person wishing to file a petition requesting the adoption, amendment or repeal of a rule by the Building Code Council shall file a written petition on a form provided by the Building Code Council and 21 copies with the Building Code Council Secretary.

2. The petition shall include the following information:

   2.1. Name, address and occupation of petitioner;

   2.2. A summary of the proposed action (adoption, amendment or repeal of a rule or rules);

   2.3. A draft of the proposed rule or other action;

2.4. A complete statement of the reason for the proposed action with supporting documentation;

2.5. An identification of the persons or class of persons most likely to be affected by the proposed action; and

2.6. An economic impact analysis as required by General Statute §143-138(a).

102.2 Presiding officer. The presiding officer at any rule-making hearing shall have control of the proceedings, including: recognition of speakers, time allotments for presentations, the right to question speakers, direction of the discussion and management of the hearing.

102.3 Record of proceedings. A record of rule-making proceedings will be available for public inspection during regular office hours at the Building Code Council's office. This record will contain the original petition, if any, the notice, all written memoranda and information submitted, and a record or summary of oral presentations, if any, and, in any case where a proposal was rejected, the reason therefore.

102.4 Effective date of rules. Any rules that are adopted by the Building Code Council and approved by the Rules Review Commission shall be effective when the next edition of the relevant technical code is effective as provided in Rule 102.6 unless specified otherwise by the Building Code Council.

102.5 Interim use of approved rules. Any rules that are adopted by the Building Code Council and approved by the Rules Review Commission shall be accepted by the Code Enforcement Official as an alternate method of construction prior to the effective date if requested by the owner or his agent.

102.6 Effective date of code editions. The provisions of any code edition which have been approved by both the Building Code Council and the Rules Review Commission shall become effective the first day of January of the following year unless specified otherwise by the Building Code Council.

SECTION 103
APPEALS

103.1 Form of complaints and other pleadings.

1. There shall be no specific form required for complaints. To be sufficient, a complaint shall be in writing, identify the parties and shall reasonably apprise the Building Code Council of the facts that form the basis of the complaint.

2. There shall be no specific form required for answers, motions or other pleadings relating to appeals before the Building Code Council, except they shall be in writing. To be sufficient, the document shall identify the case to which it refers and reasonably apprise the Building Code Council of the matters it alleges, answers or requests. In lieu of submission in writing, motions, requests and other pleadings may be made on the record during the course of the hearing before the Building Code Council.

103.2 Governing provisions. Hearings before the Building Code Council shall be governed by the provisions of General Statutes 150B, Article 3A.

103.3 Presiding officer. The Building Code Council may designate any of its members to preside over the hearing in a case on appeal. When no designation is made, the chairman of the Building Code Council shall preside, or, in his absence, the vice chairman shall preside. The presiding officer shall rule on motions or other requests made in an appeal case prior to the hearing in that case, except when the ruling on the motion would be dispositive of the case. When the ruling on a motion or request would be dispositive of the case, the presiding officer shall make no ruling and the motion or request shall be determined by a majority of the Building Code Council.

103.4 Continuances. The Building Code Council's Secretary may grant the first request for a continuance of a hearing for good cause. Any subsequent requests for continuance may be granted by the chairman of the board. The granting of a continuance is wholly discretionary.

103.5 Modifications. Whenever there are practical difficulties involved in carrying out the provisions of the technical codes, the Building Code Council shall have the authority to grant modifications for individual cases, after the Building Code Council finds on appeal that (1) special individual reasons, conditions, and/or circumstances exist that make the strict letter of the technical codes impractical, (2) the modification is in compliance with the intent and purpose of the technical codes, and (3) the modification does not lessen health, accessibility, life, fire-safety or structural requirements.

> *Commentary: Limitation on what constitutes practical difficulties. This section is not intended to permit setting aside or ignoring a code provision; rather, it is intended to provide for the acceptance of equivalent protection. Such modifications do not, however, extend to actions that are necessary to correct violations of the code. In other words, a code violation or the expense of correcting a code violation does not necessarily constitute a practical difficulty.*

SECTION 104
ADMINISTRATION

104.1 North Carolina Department of Insurance, Engineering Division.

104.1.1 Document approval. Construction specifications and drawings, including Appendix B of this code, for buildings specified in Table 104.1 shall be submitted to the Engineering Division of the North Carolina Department of Insurance. The Engineering Division shall grant document approval before a permit is issued on any building listed in Table 104.1.

TABLE 104.1
NORTH CAROLINA DEPARTMENT OF INSURANCE, ENGINEERING DIVISION DOCUMENT APPROVAL FOR NEW CONSTRUCTION AND ADDITIONS

OCCUPANCY GROUP	BUILDING PLANS TO BE APPROVED
Section 403 – High Rise[1]	All buildings
Section 402 – Covered Mall Buildings[1]	All buildings
City/county owned	All buildings 20,000 sq. ft. or greater as required by G.S. §58-31-40
Group A[1,2]	Occupant load over 1,000
Group E[1]	Over 2 stories or over 20,000 sq. ft./story
Group H[1]	Occupant load over 100
Group I[1]	Over 3 stories or over 10,000 sq. ft./story
Group R[1]	Over 4 stories or over 100 units/building

For SI: 1 square foot = 0.0929 m².

1. Plans and specifications are not required by the Engineering Division on buildings, except city/county owned, that are located in a city or county inspection jurisdiction approved to perform plans review.
2. Except temporary bleachers.

Commentary: The square footage listed above refers to the footprint of a new building or building addition.

The occupant loads refer to a new building or building addition area only.

For the purpose of this table only, the occupant load for a church is based on the occupant load of the Occupant Group A-3 main meeting area. If the A-3 area is over 1,000 occupants, then DOI plan review is required unless exception 2 applies.

General Statute 58-31-40 indicates that such city/county-owned buildings must be greater than 20,000 square feet (1858 m²) of new or additional building footprint to require DOI review. The 20,000 square feet (1858 m²) applies to individual structures on the site and not the sum of the structures.

104.1.2 Local plan review approval.

1. An inspection department may make a written request to the Building Code Council to review plans and specifications on buildings listed in Table 104.1. This authority shall be granted provided that the inspection department is adequately staffed by code enforcement officials with Standard Level III Certificates issued by the North Carolina Code Officials Qualification Board in all areas.

2. Local inspection departments approved under this section shall be listed on the Department of Insurance web page, or a list shall be provided by the Building Code Council Secretary. www.ncdoi.com/osfm.

SECTION 105
ALTERNATE MATERIAL, DESIGN OR METHODS

105.1 Approval. The provisions of this code are intended to allow the use of any alternate material, design or method of construction, provided that the alternate has been approved by the code enforcement official. An alternative material, design or method of construction shall be approved where the code enforcement official finds that the proposed alternative material, design or method of construction complies with the intent and provisions of the technical codes.

Commentary: The technical codes are not intended to inhibit innovative ideas or technological advances. A comprehensive regulatory document, such as the North Carolina Building Codes, cannot envision and then address all future innovations in the industry. As a result, a performance code must be applicable to and provide a basis for the approval of an increasing number of newly developed, innovative materials, systems and methods for which no code text or referenced standards yet exist. The fact that a material, product or method of construction is not addressed in the technical codes is not an indication that such material, product or method is intended to be prohibited. The code enforcement official is expected to apply sound technical judgment in accepting materials, systems or methods that, while not anticipated by the drafters of the current code text, can be demonstrated to offer equivalent performance. By virtue of its text, the code regulates new and innovative construction practices while addressing the relative safety of building occupants. The code enforcement official is responsible for determining if a requested alternative provides the equivalent level of protection of public health, safety and welfare as required by the code.

105.2 Tests or analysis. Whenever there is insufficient evidence of compliance with the provisions of the technical codes, or evidence that a material, design or method does not conform to the requirements of the technical codes, or in order to substantiate claims for an alternative material, design or method, the code enforcement official shall have the authority to require tests as evidence of compliance to be made at no expense to the authority having jurisdiction. Test methods shall be as specified in the technical codes or by other recognized test standards. In the absence of recognized and accepted test methods, the code enforcement official shall approve the testing procedures.

SECTION 106
PERMITS

106.1 Permit required. A current permit is required for all work described in the technical codes unless specifically exempted by the North Carolina General Statutes or the technical codes.

> *Commentary: Reference North Carolina General Statutes §153A-357 and §160A-417 for exemptions.*

106.2 Drawings and Specifications.

106.2.1 Requirements. Drawings and specifications, as required by the inspection department, shall be drawn to scale with sufficient clarity and detail to indicate the nature and character of the work and shall accompany the application for a permit. All information, drawings, specifications and accompanying data shall bear the name, address and signature of the person responsible for the design.

106.2.2 Additional data. The inspection department may require details, computations, stress diagrams or documentation sealed by a registered design professional and other data necessary to describe the construction or installation of a system.

106.2.3 Review and approval. When the inspection department issues a permit, it shall approve, in writing or by stamp, all sets of drawings and specifications "Reviewed for Code Compliance."

> **Exception:** Nothing in this section shall require the review and approval of one- and two-family dwelling plans.

> *Commentary: Drawings and specifications shall be kept in a manner prescribed by North Carolina General Statutes §153A-373 and §160A-433.*

SECTION 107
INSPECTIONS

107.1 General. The inspection department shall perform the following inspections:

1. Footing inspection;
2. Under slab inspection, as appropriate;
3. Foundation inspection, wood-frame construction;
4. Rough-in inspection;
5. Building framing;
6. Insulation inspection;
7. Fire protection inspection; and
8. Final inspection.

107.1.1 Footing inspection. Footing inspections shall be made after the trenches are excavated, all grade stakes are installed, all reinforcing steel and supports are in place and appropriately tied, all necessary forms are in place and braced and before any concrete is placed.

107.1.2 Under-slab inspection. Under-slab inspections, as appropriate, shall be made after all materials and equipment to be concealed by the concrete slab are completed.

107.1.3 Foundation inspection, crawl space. Foundation and crawl space inspections shall be made after all foundation supports are installed. This inspection is to check foundation supports, crawl space leveling, ground clearances and positive drainage when required.

107.1.4 Rough-in inspection. Rough-in inspections shall be made when all building framing and parts of the electrical, plumbing, fire protection, or heating-ventilation or cooling system that will be hidden from view in the finished building have been placed but before any wall, ceiling finish or building insulation is installed.

107.1.5 Building framing inspection. Framing inspections shall be made after the roof, excluding permanent roof covering, wall ceiling and floor framing is complete with appropriate blocking, bracing and firestopping in place. The following items shall be in place and visible for inspection:

1. Pipes;
2. Chimneys and vents;
3. Flashing for roofs, chimneys and wall openings;
4. Insulation baffles; and
5. All lintels that are required to be bolted to the framing for support shall not be covered by any exterior or interior wall or ceiling finish material before approval. Work may continue without approval for lintels supported on masonry or concrete.

107.1.6 Insulation inspection. Insulation inspections shall be made after an approved building framing and rough-in inspection and after the permanent roof covering is installed, with all insulation and vapor retarders in place, but before any wall or ceiling covering is applied.

107.1.7 Fire protection inspection. Fire protection inspections shall be made in all buildings where any material is used for fire protection purposes. The permit holder or his agent shall notify the inspection department after all fire protection materials are in place. Fire protection materials shall not be concealed until inspected and approved by the code enforcement official.

107.1.8 Final inspection. Final inspections shall be made for each trade after completion of the work authorized under the technical codes.

107.2 Inspection requests. It shall be the duty of the permit holder or his or her agent to notify the code enforcement official when work is ready for inspection and to provide access to and means for inspection of the work for any inspections that are required by this code.

107.3 Approval required. Work shall not be done beyond the point indicated in each successive inspection without first obtaining the approval of the code enforcement official. The code enforcement official, upon notification, shall make the requested inspections and shall either indicate the portion of the construction that is satisfactory as completed, or shall notify the permit holder or an agent of the permit holder that the work fails to comply with the technical codes. The code enforcement official shall identify code violations and when requested shall identify the specific sections of the technical codes. Any work that does not comply shall be corrected and shall not be covered or concealed until authorized by the code enforcement official.

107.4 Independent inspections authorized by the code enforcement official. The code enforcement official may authorize a North Carolina registered design professional to inspect the following structural elements, components and systems:

1. The excavation of soil and/or forming of footings with the associated placement of reinforcing steel prior to pouring concrete; and

2. The forming of floors, columns, beams and other structural members, including the placement of reinforcing steel prior to pouring concrete.

To utilize this procedure, the permit holder must continue to schedule all inspections normally required for this work by the inspection department. The registered design professional shall provide weekly reports bearing his seal to the inspection department indicating that the placement of the related construction elements, components and systems either complies or does not comply with the approved permit documents. Any change from the permit documents shall be approved by the code enforcement official prior to its implementation. The permit holder shall immediately inform the code enforcement official if he or she terminates his or her relationship with the registered design professional.

107.5 Special inspections. Special inspections required by the building code or the building inspector shall be performed by a North Carolina registered design professional or an inspector under his responsible charge.

> *Commentary: Special inspections are code-required inspections that are beyond the scope of inspections performed by building code inspectors. These special inspections are found only in the Building Code at this time.*
>
> *The reports required in Section 1704 of the building code would require the seals for the responsible special inspector(s).*

CHAPTER 2
ADMINISTRATIVE POLICIES

SECTION 201
SCOPE

201.1 Scope. Chapter 2 is provided as procedural policies. Items discussed in this chapter are intended as commentary to the General Statutes.

SECTION 202
BUILDING CODE COUNCIL

www.ncbuildingcodes.com

202.1 Duties. The Building Code Council has the following duties:

1. Prepare and adopt the North Carolina Building Code;

2. Revise or amend the code;

3. Hear appeals from decisions of state enforcement agencies as to any matter related to the code;

4. Make a thorough and continuing study of the manner of enforcement of the code and building laws;

5. Make recommendations to State agencies about any changes in administrative practices which could improve the enforcement of the code or building laws; and

6. Recommend to the General Assembly statutory changes to simplify and improve the building laws.

(General Statutes 143-138, 143-140 and 143-142)

202.2 Composition. The Building Code Council shall consist of 17 members appointed by the governor as follows:

1 and 2.   Two registered architects;

3. One licensed general contractor;

4. One licensed general contractor specializing in residential construction;

5. One licensed general contractor specializing in coastal residential construction;

6. One licensed engineer practicing structural engineering;

7. One licensed engineer practicing mechanical engineering;

8. One licensed engineer practicing electrical engineering;

9. One licensed plumbing and heating contractor;

10. One municipal or county building inspector;

11. One representative of the public who is not a member of the building construction industry;

12. One licensed electrical contractor;

13. One licensed engineer on the engineering staff of a State agency charged with approval of plans of State-owned buildings;

14. One representative of the fire services;

15. One licensed liquid petroleum gas dealer/contractor involved in the design of natural and liquified petroleum gas systems who has expertise and experience in natural and liquid petroleum gas piping, venting and appliances;

16. One municipal elected official or city manager; and

17. One county commissioner or county manager.

(General Statute 143-136)

202.3 Officers and committees. The Building Code Council shall elect a chairman and vice chairman from its appointed members. The officers shall serve for a period of two years from the date of election or until their successors are elected. The Building Code Council shall appoint a person to serve as secretary to the Building Code Council from the Engineering Division of the Department of Insurance.

(General Statute 143-137)

202.4 Meetings. The Building Code Council shall meet at least every 6 months. Special meetings may be called by the chairman. Any seven members of the Building Code Council shall constitute a quorum. Information concerning the exact time and place of each meeting shall be made available from the Engineering Division of the Department of Insurance 15 days prior to each such meeting. Agenda items, other than proposed amendments, must be submitted to the Building Code Council Secretary 21 days prior to the scheduled meeting.

(General Statute 143-137)

202.5 Proposed amendments. The Building Code Council may revise or amend the code, either on its own motion or upon application from any person, state agency or political subdivision of the state. Each request to amend the code shall comply with the following policies of the Building Code Council:

202.5.1 Twenty-one copies of the proposed amendment with supporting documentation shall be filed with the Building Code Council Secretary.

202.5.2 The filing shall be received by the first day of the month prior to the quarterly scheduled meeting date.

202.5.3 Each request shall be legibly printed, typed or copied on a form (see Appendix C) available from the North Carolina Department of Insurance, Building Code Council section and shall contain the following:

1. The proposed amendment must be set forth in full and contain an explicit reference to the affected section or sections of the code;

2. The request shall state the reasons for the proposed amendment with supporting documentation;

3. The proposed amendment shall comply with the standards set forth in General Statute 143-138(c) and ref-

erence to the particular standards shall be set forth in the request for the amendment; and

4. The proposed amendment shall contain an economic impact analysis as required by General Statute 143-138(a).

202.5.4 When a request is improperly filed or not in accordance with all the rules listed above, the Building Code Council Secretary shall reject the submittal and notify the applicant of the proper procedure to follow.

202.5.5 Upon the proper filing of a request, the Building Code Council Secretary shall forward one copy of said request to each council member prior to the scheduled meeting date. Persons filing proposed petitions are hereby notified of the place and time of the scheduled hearings. The Building Code Council Secretary shall cause to be published the notice of public hearing as specified in North Carolina General Statutes 143-138(a).

202.5.6 The Building Code Council shall either grant or deny the proposed petition for rule-making at the meeting following receipt of the proposed rule change. The council will take no further action on items that are denied. Granted items may be referred to committee for review.

202.5.7 The Building Code Council may hold a public hearing on granted items at the next quarterly scheduled meeting. The council may take final action on granted items at the next quarterly scheduled meeting after the public hearing.

Timeline Example

Petition Received:	February 1
Petition Granted:	March BCC meeting
Notice of Hearing Published:	April NC Register
Committee Review:	April - May
Hearing Held:	June BCC meeting
Final Adoption:	September BCC meeting
Rules Review Meeting:	November RRC meeting
Approved:	December 1

202.6 Publications.

202.6.1 Amendments. The Building Code Council shall print all amendments to the codes, and the amendments shall be available for distribution in accordance with General Statute 143-138(g). Notices and minutes are available either at no charge on the Council web page or for a fee as prescribed by Agency Rules.

202.6.2 Council webpage. The minutes and agenda of the Building Code Council may be found on the Council web page located at http://www.ncbuildingcodes.com. Click on the desired information topic.

202.6.3 Engineering newsletter. Newsletters will be sent to online subscribers. Archive copies may be found on the Engineering web page located at http://www.ncdoi.com/osfm. Click on Building Codes to subscribe.

202.7 Approval of local ordinances. The Building Code Council may approve local regulations governing the Fire Prevention Code. All regulations shall be approved by the Building Code Council in order to be legally effective. Regulations approved by the local governing body, which are found to be more stringent than the fire prevention code and, which are found to regulate activities and conditions in buildings, structures, and premises that pose dangers of fire, explosion or related hazards, and are not in conflict with the North Carolina Building Code, shall be approved once reviewed and filed by the Building Code Council. The rules listed in Section 202.5 shall apply for filing a proposed local deviation to the Fire Prevention Code along with the following:

1. Twenty-one copies of the resolution adopted by the governing body requesting the proposed deviation to the fire prevention code.

2. After approval by the Building Code Council, the Building Code Council Secretary shall advise the local governing body and shall retain a copy in the Building Code Council's file as a permanent record.

[General Statute 143-138(e)]

202.8 Committees.

202.8.1 Standing committees. The standing committees shall consist of members of the Building Code Council. The Chairman of the Building Code Council shall appoint the chairmen and members of each committee.

202.8.2 Ad hoc committees. For each code edition, the Chairman shall establish and appoint ad hoc code revision committees and appoint the chairmen. The ad hoc committees shall consider and prepare revisions and amendments to the code volumes. Each ad hoc committee shall consist of members of the Building Code Council, Department of Insurance staff, licensed contractors, and design professionals most affected by the code volume for which the ad hoc committee is responsible and members of the public.

> *Guidelines for Ad Hoc Committees:*
>
> *1. Ad Hoc committee is asked to approach its code review with the idea of producing a newly amended code with as few changes from the 2009 ICC as the committee deems practicable.*
>
> *2. Current Code shall be considered base line for code comparison.*
>
> *3. Ad Hoc committee is asked to provide a list of major changes to the Standing Committee and Council for review.*
>
> *4. If code changes are thought to be controversial, it is suggested that the Ad Hoc committee consider handling such items as separate stand alone code changes.*
>
> *5. Ad Hoc committees shall submit its report to the appropriate Standing Committee for review.*
>
> *6. After its review, the Standing Committee is asked to make a recommendation to the Building Code Council for adoption.*

202.8.3 Hearing committee. The chairman may appoint a hearing committee to hear an appeal.

202.9 Appeals.

202.9.1 Engineering division. A written technical interpretation shall be provided as specified in Section 203.1.2.1.2. Any person may appeal in writing an order, decision or determination pertaining to the code or any state building law by filing written notice with the Commissioner of Insurance or his designee within 10 days after the order, decision or determination. A copy of the appeal shall be furnished to each party.

(General Statutes 143-140, 153A-374 and 160A-434)

202.9.2 Building Code Council. The Building Code Council shall hear appeals from the decisions of state enforcement agencies relating to any matter related to the code. Any person wishing to appeal a decision of a state enforcement agency to the Building Code Council shall give written notice of appeal as follows:

202.9.2.1 Twenty-one copies including an original of the Notice of Appeal shall be filed with the Building Code Council c/o North Carolina Department of Insurance, Engineering Division, 322 Chapanoke Road, Suite 200, Raleigh, North Carolina 27603, and one copy shall be filed with the state enforcement agency from which the appeal is taken.

202.9.2.2 The Notice of Appeal shall be received no later than 30 days from the date of the decision of the State enforcement agency.

202.9.2.3 The Notice of Appeal shall be legibly printed, typewritten or copied and shall contain the following (See Appendix E):

1. Name, address of the party or parties requesting the appeal.
2. The name of the state enforcement agency, the date of the decision from which the appeal is taken, and a copy of the written decision received from the enforcement agency.
3. The decision from which the appeal is taken shall be set forth in full in the Notice of Appeal or a copy of the decision shall be attached to all copies of the Notice of Appeal.
4. The contentions and allegations of fact must be set forth in full in a clear and concise manner with reference to the sections of the code in controversy.
5. The original Notice of Appeal shall be signed by the party or parties filing appeal.
6. The Notice of Appeal shall be received by the first day of the month prior to the Building Code Council's quarterly scheduled meeting in order to be placed on the agenda for that meeting. The Chairman may schedule a special meeting to hear an appeal.

202.9.2.4 Upon the proper filing of the Notice of Appeal, the Building Code Council Secretary shall forward one copy of the Notice of Appeal to each member of the Building Code Council. The chairman may appoint a Hearing Committee to hear appeals. The Secretary shall send notice in writing to the party or parties requesting an appeal and to the Building Code Council Hearing Committee members at least 15 days prior to the Hearing Committee meeting. A written decision of the Hearing Committee meeting shall be provided to all Building Code Council Members. The actions of the Hearing Committee shall be final, unless appealed to the full Building Code Council in writing within 30 days of the Hearing Committee's action. If a Hearing Committee consists of at least seven council members, it will constitute a quorum of the full council. Further appeals shall be as specified in Section 202.9.3.

202.9.2.5 The Building Code Council shall, upon a motion of the State enforcement agency or on its own motion, dismiss appeals for the following reasons:

1. Not pursued by the appellant or withdrawn;
2. Appeal not filed in accordance with these rules; or
3. Lack of jurisdiction.

202.9.2.6 When the Building Code Council finds that a State enforcement agency was in error in its interpretation of the code, the Building Code Council shall remand the case to the agency with instructions to take such actions as the Building Code Council directs. When the Building Code Council finds on appeal that materials or methods of construction proposed are equivalent to those required by the code, the Building Code Council shall remand the case to the state enforcement agency with instructions to permit the use of such materials or methods of construction. The Building Code Council shall immediately initiate procedures for amending the code to permit the use of such materials or methods of construction.

202.9.2.7 The Building Code Council shall provide a written decision setting forth the findings of fact and the Building Code Council's conclusions to each party or parties filing the appeal and to the State enforcement agency from which the appeal was taken.

202.9.3 Superior court. Whenever any person desires to appeal a decision of the Building Code Council or a decision of a State or local enforcement agency, he may appeal either to the Wake County Superior Court or the superior court of the county in which the proposed building is to be situated in accordance with the provisions of Chapter 150B of the General Statutes.

[General Statute 143-141(d)]

SECTION 203
NORTH CAROLINA DEPARTMENT OF INSURANCE
www.ncdoi.com/osfm

203.1 Administration.

203.1.1 Commissioner of Insurance. The Commissioner of Insurance through the Engineering Division shall have general supervision of the administration and enforcement of the North Carolina State Building Code. This includes all sections of the code pertaining to:

1. General building restrictions and regulations;

2. Plumbing;

3. Heating and air conditioning;

4. Electrical systems;

5. Fire protection; and

6. Natural or liquified petroleum gas systems.

[General Statute 143-139 (b)]

203.1.1.1 Investigation of fires. Whenever the Commissioner of Insurance has reason to believe that investigators of fire or fire prevention inspectors are not fulfilling their responsibilities, he or his designee shall take proper steps to have all provisions of the law enforced.

(General Statute 58-2-95)

203.1.1.2 Investigation of premises for dangerous materials. The Commissioner of Insurance or his or her designee shall hear appeals from orders issued by the code enforcement official to remove or remedy combustible materials or inflammable conditions dangerous to any building or premises. The appeal shall be made within 24 hours of issue, not counting weekends or holidays. The commissioner shall cause the complaint to be investigated immediately. The Commissioner or his or her designee may make inspections of the complaint alone or in the company of the code enforcement official. Unless the Commissioner by his or her authority revokes the order of the code enforcement official, the order remains in force and must be complied with by the owner or occupant.

(General Statute 58-79-20)

203.1.1.3 Buildings within primary fire limits. The Commissioner of Insurance or his or her designee shall review all permits to erect, alter, repair or move any wood-frame building or structure within the primary fire district of a municipality. Such permits shall be received and approved by the Inspection Department and approved by the Municipal Council prior to the Commissioner or his or her designee's approval.

(General Statutes 153A-375 and 160A-436)

203.2 Engineering Division. The Engineering Division of the Department of Insurance shall serve as staff for the Building Code Council and the Code Official's Qualification Board. The Engineering Division shall work in cooperation with code enforcement officials and provide general supervision in the administration and interpretation of the codes. The staff shall handle correspondence and maintain an accurate and complete record of:

1. All meetings or hearings,

2. Laboratory studies, and

3. Technical work performed by or for the Building Code Council.

All records shall be available for public inspection during regular office hours. All funds for the operation of the Building Code Council shall be appropriated to the Department of Insurance. The Department of Insurance may hire additional staff as may be necessary to handle the work of the Building Code Council with the approval of the council.

[General Statute 143-137(c)]

203.2.1 Interpretations.

203.2.1.1 Informal interpretations. The Engineering Division shall provide informal interpretations on code-related matters either by e-mail, letter or telephone. These informal interpretations may be accepted by the local code enforcement official or party requesting the interpretation. Either party may request a formal interpretation of the code.

203.2.1.2 Formal interpretations. Any person may request in writing a formal interpretation of the code. The request shall be addressed to the Chief Code Consultant for the Department of Insurance. The request shall be specific and shall reference the code sections in question. All formal interpretations shall be in writing. A formal interpretation shall be binding on all parties unless appealed to the Building Code Council as specified in Section 201.9.2. Formal interpretations determined to be of a general nature may be posted on the department web site.

(General Statute 143-140)

203.2.2 Appeals. Any person may appeal in writing an order, decision or determination of a code enforcement official pertaining to the code or any state building law. The appeal shall be addressed to the Chief Engineer for the Department of Insurance by filing written notice within 10 days after the order, decision or determination. The appeal shall contain the type and size of the building in question, the location of the building and shall reference the code sections in question. The decision shall be in writing and shall set forth the facts found. The decision rendered shall be based on the technical provisions of the code, public health and safety and shall be construed liberally to those ends. A decision shall be binding on all parties unless an appeal is submitted to the Building Code Council as specified in Section 201.9.2. A copy of the appeal and written decision shall be furnished to each party.

(General Statutes 153A-374 and 160A-434)

SECTION 204
CITY AND COUNTY GOVERNMENT

www.ncgov.com
(Click on "For Government, Local Government")

204.1 General. The powers, duties and responsibilities of the code enforcement official are generally described in the following General Statutes:

1. GS153A-352 for counties, and

2. GS160A-412 for cities.

204.2 Inspection department.

204.2.1 General. The responsibility for administration and enforcement of the code has been allocated to local code enforcement officials under the supervision of State officials as designated within Section 203.

[General Statute 143-139(b)]

204.2.2 Jurisdiction. A municipal inspection department shall have jurisdiction over all areas within the city limits, all extraterritorial areas that the city has jurisdiction pursuant to state laws, and over any areas in which the municipal limits have contracted with another unit of government to perform code enforcement. A county inspection department shall have jurisdiction over all unincorporated areas outside any municipal jurisdiction located within the county, all areas in which a municipality has requested the county to enforce the code, and within the jurisdiction of another unit of government in which the county has contracted to perform code enforcement. A joint inspection department created by two or more units of government shall have the authority to enforce the code in all areas of legal jurisdiction of all units of government supporting the joint department.

(General Statutes 153A-352 and 153A-353 for counties, and 160A-411 and 160A-413 for cities.)

204.2.3 Duties. Inspection departments shall:

1. Receive applications and supporting data for permits;

2. Issue or deny permits;

3. Make all necessary inspections to ensure code compliance;

4. Identify technical provisions found to be inconsistent with the inspection;

5. Issue or deny certificates of compliance and certificates of occupancy;

6. Issue stop work orders or orders to correct violations;

7. Maintain adequate records of permits issued or denied, inspections made, corrections ordered and certifications issued; and

8. Take other actions that may be required to adequately enforce the code.

(General Statutes 153A-352 and 160A-412)

204.2.4 Code enforcement official's qualifications. No state or local government employee shall enforce any provision of the North Carolina State Building Codes who does not possess an appropriate valid certificate issued by the North Carolina Code Official's Qualification Board as specified in General Statutes 143-151.13, 153A-351.1 and 160A-411.1.

204.2.5 Conflict of interest. Information about conflict of interest for code enforcement officials can be found in General Statutes 153A-355 for counties and 160A-415 for cities.

204.2.6 Right of entry. The code enforcement official shall have the right to enter buildings or premises as described in General Statutes 153A-360 and 153A-364 for counties, and 160A-420 and 160A-421 for cities.

204.2.7 Stop work orders. General Statute 153A-361 authorizes a county code enforcement official to issue stop work orders. General Statute 160A-421 authorizes a city code enforcement official to issue stop work orders. These statutes describe when a stop work order can be issued, how the stop work order is to be issued and how the stop work order may be appealed.

204.2.8 Unsafe building or systems. A county code enforcement official's authority to condemn an unsafe building is found in General Statute 153A-366. A city code enforcement official's authority to condemn an unsafe building is found in General Statute 160A-426.

204.3 Permits.

204.3.1 General. No person may commence or proceed with:

1. The construction, reconstruction, alteration, repair, movement to another site, removal or demolition of any building;

2. The installation, extension or general repair of any plumbing system;

3. The installation, extension, alteration or general repair of any heating or cooling equipment system; or

4. The installation, extension, alteration or general repair of any electrical wiring, devices, appliances or equipment without first securing from the Inspection Department with jurisdiction over the site of the work each permit required by the North Carolina State Building Codes and other State or local law or local ordinance or regulation applicable to the work.

(General Statute 153A-357 and 160A-417)

204.3.2 Validity. In accordance with General Statutes 153A-358 for counties and 160A-418 for cities, a permit expires 6 months, or any lesser time fixed by local ordinances, after the date of issuance if the work authorized by the permit has not been commenced. If, after commencement, the work is discontinued for a period of 12 months, the permit immediately expires. No work authorized by a permit that has expired may be performed until a new permit has been issued.

204.3.3 Changes in work. Work shall not deviate substantially from that described on the permit documents.

204.3.4 Information required. A permit application shall be filed with the Inspection Department on a form furnished for that purpose. The Inspection Department shall make available a list of information which must be submitted with the building permit application, including a complete building code summary (see Appendix B) and a permit application information sheet (see Appendix A).

204.3.5 Design professional seal required. Where the General Statutes require, no permit shall be issued unless the construction documents (drawings and specifications), bear the North Carolina seal of a registered design professional. Construction documents shall include the name and address of the business entity (individual, corporation or partnership) with whom the registered design professional is affiliated. Questions concerning this section should be directed to the North Carolina Board of Architecture or the North Carolina Board of Examiners for Engineers and Land Surveyors.

Exceptions: For permitting purposes, the seal of a registered design professional is not required when the building, structure or project involved is in one of the categories listed below, unless otherwise required pursuant to the provisions of the General Statutes or the technical codes:

1. A family residence, up to eight units attached with grade-level exit, which is not a part of or physically connected with any other buildings or residential units. More than one such set of attached units on a site is determined to be a complex and will require the seal of a registered design professional;

2. A building upon any farm that is for the use of any farmer, unless the building is of such nature and intended for such use as to substantially involve the health or safety of the public;

3. An institutional or commercial building if it does not have a total cost of construction exceeding $90,000;

4. An institutional or commercial building if the total building area does not exceed 2,500 square feet (2.32 m²) in gross floor area;

5. Alteration, remodeling or renovation of an existing building that is exempt under this section, or alteration, remodeling or renovation of an existing building or building site that does not alter or affect the structural system of the building; change the building's access or exit pattern; or change the live or dead load on the building's structural system. This subdivision shall not limit or change any other exemptions to this chapter or to the practice of engineering under Chapter 89C of the General Statutes.

6. The preparation and use of details and shop drawings, assembly or erection drawings, or graphic descriptions utilized to detail or illustrate a portion of the work required to construct the project in accordance with the plans and specifications prepared or to be prepared under the requirements or exemptions of this chapter.

7. Nothing in this chapter shall be construed to prevent any individual from making plans or data for buildings for himself or herself. This exemption does not apply to plans for places of religious worship.

204.3.5.1 Registered design professional. The registered design professional shall be a registered architect, licensed professional engineer or NICET Level III sprinkler designer legally registered or licensed under the laws of this state.

204.3.6 Contractor license required. When the General Statutes require that general construction, plumbing, mechanical, electrical, fire protection or gas work be performed by an appropriately licensed individual, no permit for such type work shall be issued to an unlicensed person or firm. Additional requirements may be found in General Statutes 87-14, 87-21(e), 87-43.1, 87-58, 153A-134, 153A-357, 160A-194 and 160A-417.

204.3.7 Contractor responsibilities. It shall be the duty of every person who contracts for the installation or repair of a building or service system to comply with State or local rules and regulations concerning licensing. It shall be the contractor's responsibility to conform to the technical codes for all installations or repairs of a building or service system.

204.4 Issuing permits.

204.4.1 Action on permits. In accordance with General Statute 153A-357 for counties and General Statute 160A-417 for cities, the Inspection Department shall examine each application for a permit to determine if it is in compliance with the requirements of the technical codes and other pertinent laws and ordinances. If the inspection department is satisfied that the work described in the application conforms to the requirements of the technical codes and other pertinent laws and ordinances, it shall issue a permit to the applicant. If the application does not conform to the requirements of the technical codes and other pertinent laws and ordinances, the application shall be returned to the applicant with the reasons for refusal stated.

(General Statutes 153A-352, 160A-412 and 160A-417)

204.4.2 Permits for modular construction. Permits shall be required for the installation, connection of units, foundations, utility connections or alterations of buildings or components manufactured off the site and labeled by a third-party agency accredited and listed by the Building Code Council.

204.4.2.1 Third-party certification agencies. Third-party certification agencies shall be accredited and listed by the Building Code Council. Inspection and certification of buildings or components manufactured off the site and labeled by a third-party agency shall be accepted by the inspection department without further inspection. Permits and fees may be required for any installation, connection of units, foundations, utility connections or alterations of such work.

204.5 Conditions of the permit.

204.5.1 Contractor responsibilities. It shall be the duty of every person who contracts for the installation or repair of a building or services system to comply with state or local rules and regulations concerning licensing. It shall be the contractor's responsibility to conform to this code and the technical codes for all installations or repairs of a building or service system. Violations and penalties of these provisions are listed in Sections 204.12 through 204.14 of this code. Additional requirements can be found in General Statutes 87-1 through 87-14.

204.5.2 Permit intent. A permit issued shall be construed as permission to proceed with the work and not as authority to violate, cancel, alter or set aside any of the provisions of the technical codes. Issuance of a permit shall not prevent the inspection department from requiring correction of errors in plans, construction or violations of this code.

(General Statutes 153A-357 and 160A-417)

204.5.3 Revocation of permits.

204.5.3.1 Misrepresentation of application. The code enforcement official shall revoke, in writing, a permit or approval issued under the provisions of this or the technical codes for:

1. Any substantial departure from the approved application, drawings or specifications;

2. Refusal or failure to comply with the requirements of any applicable State or local laws;

3. Any false statement or misrepresentation as to the material fact in the application or plans on which the permit or approval was based.

See the North Carolina Fire Prevention Code for other permit revocation requirements.

204.5.3.2 Violation of code provisions. The code enforcement official may revoke a permit upon determination that the work for which the permit was issued is in violation of, or not in conformity with, the provisions of this or the technical codes.

(General Statute 153A-362, 160A-422)

204.6 Fees.

204.6.1 Fees. A permit shall not be issued until the fees prescribed by the local governing authority have been paid. No amendment to a permit shall be released until the additional fee, if any, has been paid.

(General Statutes 153A-354 and 160A-414)

204.6.2 Work commencing before permit issuance. If any person commences any work on a building or service systems before obtaining the necessary permit, he or she shall be subject to a penalty as established by the local governing body.

(General Statutes 153A-354 and 160A-414)

204.7 Inspections.

204.7.1 Periodic inspections for hazardous or unlawful conditions. The inspection department shall make periodic inspections as specified in General Statutes 153A-364 for counties and 160A-424 for cities.

204.7.2 Required public school inspections. Inspections of schools for fire hazards shall be in accordance with General Statute 115C-525(b).

204.8 Certificate of compliance.

204.8.1 Building occupancy. A new building shall not be occupied or a change made in the occupancy, nature or use of a building or part of a building until after the inspection department has issued a certificate of compliance. The certificate of compliance shall not be issued until all required service systems have been inspected for compliance with the technical codes and other applicable laws and ordinances and released by the inspection department.

(General Statutes 153A-363 and 160A-423)

204.8.2 Certificate of compliance. Upon satisfactory completion of a building, plumbing, mechanical, electrical, fire protection or gas system, or portion thereof, a certificate of compliance shall be issued. The certificate of compliance represents that a structure or system is complete and for certain types of permits is permission granted for connection to a utility system. The certificate of compliance shall not be construed to grant authority to occupy a building.

(General Statutes 153A-363 and 160A-423)

204.8.3 Temporary/partial occupancy. A temporary/partial certificate of compliance may be issued permitting occupancy for a stated period for specific portions of a building or service system that the inspector finds safe for occupancy prior to final completion of the entire building or system.

(General Statutes 153A-363 and 160A-423)

204.8.4 Issuing certificate of occupancy. Upon satisfactory completion of a building and after the final inspection, the inspection department may issue a certificate of occupancy. The certificate of occupancy shall state the occupancy may be safely occupied.

204.8.4.1 Existing buildings. A certificate of occupancy for any existing building may be obtained by applying to the inspection department and supplying the information and data necessary to determine compliance with the technical codes for the occupancy intended. Where necessary, the code enforcement official may require detailed drawings and inspections to determine compliance with the applicable codes. When, upon examination and inspection, it is found that the building conforms to the provisions of the technical codes and other applicable laws and ordinances for such occupancy, a certificate of occupancy shall be issued. The certificate shall state the approved occupancy type.

204.9 Service utilities.

204.9.1 Connection of service utilities. No person shall make connections from a utility, source of energy, fuel or power to any building or system that is regulated by the technical codes until approved by the inspection department and a certificate of compliance is issued.

(General Statute 143-143.2)

204.9.2 Temporary connection. The inspection department may authorize the temporary connection of the building or system to the utility source of energy, fuel or power for the purpose of testing building service systems.

(General Statutes 153A-363 and 160A-423)

204.10 Stop work orders. Whenever a stop order has been issued by an inspection department involving alleged violations of the State Building Codes, the owner or builder may appeal in writing to the Commissioner of Insurance, or his or her designee, within 5 days after the date the order is issued, with a copy of the appeal to the inspection department. No further work may take place in violation of a stop order. The Commissioner, or his or her designee, shall promptly conduct an investigation. The inspection department and the owner or builder shall be permitted to submit relevant evidence for the investigation. The Commissioner of Insurance, or his or her designee, shall provide a written statement of the decision setting forth the facts found, the decision reached and the reasons for the decision. In the event of dissatisfaction with the decision, the person affected shall have the option of appealing as set forth in Section 203.1.2.

(General Statutes 153A-361 and 160A-421)

204.11 Floor loads and occupant loads.

204.11.1 Occupancy. No building shall be occupied for any purpose that will cause the floors to be loaded beyond their safe capacity. It shall be the responsibility of the owner or occupant of any building, where excessive floor loading is likely to occur, to employ a design professional in computing the safe load capacity. The computations shall be filed as a permanent record of the inspection department. The inspection department may permit occupancy of a building when the department is satisfied that the capacity will not be exceeded.

204.11.2 Occupant load posted. When required by the code enforcement official, signs stating the occupant load determined in accordance with occupant load specified in the technical codes shall be posted by the owner of the building in each assembly room, auditorium or room used for a similar purpose where fixed seats are not installed. The seating capacity shall be determined in accordance with the technical codes and signs posted at locations approved by the code enforcement official. It shall be unlawful to remove or deface such notice or to permit more than this legal number of people within such space. The signs shall read as follows:

"Occupancy by more than _____persons is dangerous and unlawful.

_____, CEO"

204.12 Violations. Any person, firm, corporation or agent who violates a provision of this code or the technical codes shall be guilty of a Class 3 misdemeanor. Each person shall be considered guilty of a separate offense for each and every portion thereof during which any violation is committed or continued, for a period of 30 days. Upon conviction of any such violation the person shall be liable to a fine not to exceed $50.00 for each offense. Any violation incurred more than 1 year after another conviction for violation of the occupancy limits shall be treated as a first offense for the purposes of establishing and imposing penalties.

[General Statute 143-138(h)]

204.13 Remedies.

204.13.1 General. In case any building or structure is constructed or its purpose altered so that it becomes in violation of the technical codes, or if the occupancy limits established are exceeded, the code enforcement official may institute any appropriate action or proceedings, including civil remedies, to:

1. Prevent the unlawful erection, construction or reconstruction or alteration of purpose, or overcrowding;

2. Restrain, correct or abate the violation; or

3. Prevent the occupancy or use of the building, structure or land until the violation is corrected.

204.13.2 Fire prevention. Refer to the North Carolina Fire Prevention Code for summary abatement requirements for fire prevention code violations and penalties.

204.14 Code enforcement official not fulfilling responsibilities. When the code enforcement official does not fulfill his responsibilities as specified in Section 204.13, the Commissioner of Insurance or his or her designee may institute any appropriate actions or proceedings available.

(General Statutes 14-230, 14-231, 14-232, 153A-356 and l60A-41)

SECTION 205
OTHER AGENCIES
www.ncgov.com
(Click on NC Agencies)

205.1 Administration by the North Carolina Department of Labor.

205.1.1 Commissioner of Labor. The Commissioner of Labor shall have general supervision over the Elevator and Amusement Device Division and the Boiler Pressure Vessel Division.

[General Statute 143-139(c)]

205.1.2 Elevator and amusement device division. The Elevator and Amusement Device Division shall enforce the provisions of the North Carolina State Building Code that pertain to the operation of:

1. Elevators;

2. Dumbwaiters;

3. Escalators;

4. Moving walks;

5. Personnel hoists;

6. Chair and wheelchair lifts;

7. Manlifts;

8. Special equipment; and

9. Amusement devices.

Exceptions:

1. Devices and equipment located and operated within a single-family residence.

2. Equipment constructed, installed and used exclusively for the movement of materials.

3. Mining equipment covered by either the Federal Mine Safety and Health Act or the Mine Safety and Health Act of North Carolina.

[General Statute 143-139(d)]

205.1.3 Boiler and pressure vessel division. The Boiler and Pressure Vessel Division shall enforce the provisions of Chapter 95 of the General Statutes which pertain to boilers and pressure vessels. The Boiler and Pressure Vessel Division shall not regulate hot water supply boilers equipped with ASME Code and National Board certified safety relief valves, which are fired with oil, gas, or electricity or hot water supply tanks heated by any indirect means which do not exceed any of the following limitations:

1. Heat input of 200,000 Btu/hr;

2. Water temperature of 200°F (93°C);

3. Nominal water capacity of 120 gallons (454 L).

[General Statutes 95-69.10(c), 143-139(c)]

CHAPTER 3

REPRINT OF THE GENERAL STATUTES PERTAINING TO THE ENFORCEMENT OF THE NORTH CAROLINA STATE BUILDING CODE

The North Carolina State Building Codes do not include all additional requirements for buildings and structures that may be imposed by other State agencies, occupational licensing boards and commissions. It shall be the responsibility of a permit holder, design professional, contractor or occupational license holder to determine whether any additional requirements exist.

The current language of the General Statutes may be viewed at www.ncleg.net.

The following list, while extensive, may not include all applicable General Statutes.

1-539.2	Dismantling portion of building
14-68	Failure of owner of property to comply with orders of public authorities
14-228–232	Misconduct in public office
14-414	Pyrotechnics defined; exceptions
15-27.2	Administrative search and inspection warrants
42 Article 5	Landlord Tenant
58-2-95	Commissioner to supervise local inspectors
58-31-40	Commissioner to inspect state property; plans submitted
58-79-20	Inspection of premises; dangerous material removed
66-23–27	Electrical materials, devices, appliances and equipment
83A-1–13	Architects
87-1–15	General contractors
87-21	Plumbing, heating and fire sprinkler contractor
87-43	Electrical contractors
87-57–58	Refrigeration contractors
89C-3–23	Engineers
95-69	Uniform boiler and pressure vessel act
105-130–151	Accessibility tax credit
106-581.1	Agriculture Defined
115C-525	Public schools
119 Article 5	Liquefied petroleum gases
130A-336–339	Wastewater system construction
133-1–4	Public works
143-135.1	Inspection of state owned buildings
143-136–143	Building Code Council and Building Code
143-151.8–21	Code officials qualification board
143-151.42	Prohibition of master meters for electric and natural gas service
143-151.43–64	North Carolina home inspector board
150B-18–21	Administrative Procedures Act
153A-97–375	Counties
160A-167–438	Cities

PERMIT APPLICATION INFORMATION SHEET

The following information is required on all permit applications. Additional information may be included to ensure that all state and local laws are complied with. This information may be arranged in any order and the following outline is only the minimum information required.

City/County Name _____

Inspection Department _____

Permit Application _____

Applicant Name _____   Date ___ / ___ / ___

Project Address _____

Total Project Cost _____   Electrical Cost _____

Subdivision _____   Block # _____   Lot # _____

Developer _____   Phone # (_____) _____ - _____   E-Mail _____

Property Owner _____   Phone # (_____) _____ - _____   E-Mail _____

Address _____   City _____   State ___   ZIP _____

Project Contact _____   Phone # (_____) _____ - _____   E-Mail _____

Address _____   City _____   State ___   ZIP _____

Description of Proposed Work _____

Type of Building: ___New   ___Existing   ___Addition   ___N/A

Type of Construction: ___IA   ___IB   ___IIA   ___IIB   ___IIIA   ___IIIB   ___IV   ___VA   ___VB

Occupancy: ___A-1   ___A-2   ___A-3   ___A-4   ___A-5   ___B   ___E   ___F-1   ___F-2

___H-1   ___H-2   ___H-3   ___H-4   ___H-5   ___I-1   ___I-2   ___I-3   ___I-4

___M   ___R-1   ___R-2   ___R-3   ___R-4   ___S-1   ___S-2   ___U

Equipment: ___New   ___Existing   ___Addition   ___N/A

Property Use: ___Single Family   ___Two Family   ___Townhouse

___Apartment   ___Condominium

___Other (Library, Office, Etc.)

Building Area: Total Area (sf) _____   Area per floor (sf) _____

Building Height: Feet _____   # of Stories _____

State Agency Approvals:

NC Department of Insurance   ___Yes   ___No   ___N/A

Plan Approval___   # of Sheets ___   Date ___ / ___ / ___

Specifications ___   # of Sheets ___   Date ___ / ___ / ___

NC Department of Labor   ___Yes   ___No   ___N/A

Elevators ___   Date ___ / ___ / ___   Boilers ___   Date ___ / ___ / ___

Utilities Approvals:

Water: ___Public   ___Private   ___Private Health Dept. Permit # _____

Sewer: ___Public   ___Private   ___Private Health Dept. Permit # _____

Place X and complete additional information for each permit type needed.

___General Construction Permit

Contractor Name _____   Phone # (_____) _____ - _____   E-Mail _____

Address _____   City _____ State _____   ZIP _____

License # _____   Classification _____

Design Professional _____   Phone # (_____) _____ - _____   E-Mail _____

____Architect   ____Engineer   NC Reg. # _____

____Owner   ____Other

Address _____   City _____ State _____   ZIP _____

___Electrical Permit

Contractor Name _____   Phone # (_____) _____ - _____   E-Mail _____

Address _____   City _____ State _____   ZIP _____

License # _____   Classification _____

Design Professional _____   Phone # (_____) _____ - _____   E-Mail _____

____Architect   ____Engineer   NC Reg. # _____

____Owner   ____Other

Address _____   City _____ State _____   ZIP _____

___Mechanical Permit

Contractor Name _____   Phone # (_____) _____ - _____   E-Mail _____

Address _____   City _____ State _____   ZIP _____

License # _____   Classification _____

Design Professional _____   Phone # (_____) _____ - _____   E-Mail _____

____Architect   ____Engineer   NC Reg. # _____

____Owner   ____Other

Address _____   City _____ State _____   ZIP _____

___Plumbing Permit

Contractor Name _____   Phone # (_____) _____ - _____   E-Mail _____

Address _____   City _____ State _____   ZIP _____

License # _____   Classification _____

Design Professional _____   Phone # (_____) _____ - _____   E-Mail _____

____Architect   ____Engineer   NC Reg. # _____

____Owner   ____Other

Address _____   City _____ State _____   ZIP _____

___Sprinkler Protection Permit

Contractor Name _____   Phone # (_____) _____ - _____   E-Mail _____

Address _____   City _____ State _____   ZIP _____

License # _____   Classification _____

Design Professional _____   Phone # (_____) _____ - _____   E-Mail _____

____Architect   ____Engineer   NC Reg. # _____

____Owner   ____Other

Address _____   City _____ State _____   ZIP _____

___Fire Alarm System Permit

Contractor Name _____   Phone # (_____) _____ - _____   E-Mail _____

Address _____   City _____ State _____   ZIP _____

License # _____   Classification _____

Design Professional _____   Phone # (_____) _____ - _____   E-Mail _____

____Architect   ____Engineer   NC Reg. # _____

____Owner   ____Other

Address _____   City _____ State _____   ZIP _____

Place X and complete additional information for each permit type needed.

___**Sign Permit**

Location of Sign _____   Address _____

____Off Premises Sign   ____Wall Sign   ____Ground Sign   ____Awning Sign

____Projection Sign   ____Special Event Sign ____Other

Sign/Business Owner_____   Phone # (_____) _____ - _____   E-Mail _____

Address _____   City _____ State _____   ZIP _____

Contractor Name _____   Phone # (_____) _____ - _____   E-Mail _____

Address _____   City _____ State _____   ZIP _____

___**Accessory Structures Permit**

___Accessory Building   ___Size   _____ Sq.ft.

___Solid Fence   ___Dish Antenna   ___Swimming Pool   ___Other

I hereby certify that all information in this application is correct and all work will comply with the State Building Code and all other applicable State and local laws and ordinances and regulations. The Inspection Department will be notified of any changes in the approved plans and specifications for the project permitted herein.

Owner/Agent Signature _____

APPENDIX B

2012 BUILDING CODE SUMMARY
FOR ALL COMMERCIAL PROJECTS

(EXCEPT ONE- AND TWO-FAMILY DWELLINGS AND TOWNHOUSES)

(Reproduce the following data on the building plans sheet 1 or 2)

Name of Project: _____

Address: _____ Zip Code _____

Proposed Use: _____

Owner/Authorized Agent: _____ Phone # (____) _____ - _____ E-Mail _____

Owned By: ❑ City/County ❑ Private ❑ State

Code Enforcement Jurisdiction: ❑ City_____ ❑ County_____ ❑ State

---

LEAD DESIGN PROFESSIONAL: _____

DESIGNER	FIRM	NAME	LICENSE #	TELEPHONE #	E-MAIL
Architectural				(___)	
Civil				(___)	
Electrical				(___)	
Fire Alarm				(___)	
Plumbing				(___)	
Mechanical				(___)	
Sprinkler-Standpipe				(___)	
Structural				(___)	
Retaining Walls >5' High				(___)	
Other				(___)	

2012 EDITION OF NC CODE FOR: ❑ New Construction ❑ Addition ❑ Upfit

EXISTING: ❑ Reconstruction ❑ Alteration ❑ Repair ❑ Renovation

CONSTRUCTED: (date) _____ **ORIGINAL USE(S)** (Ch. 3): _____

RENOVATED: (date) _____ **CURRENT USE(S)** (Ch. 3): _____

PROPOSED USE(S) (Ch. 3): _____

BUILDING DATA

Construction Type: ❑ I-A ❑ II-A ❑ III-A ❑ IV ❑ V-A

(check all that apply) ❑ I-B ❑ II-B ❑ III-B ❑ V-B

Sprinklers: ❑ No ❑ Partial ❑ Yes ❑ NFPA 13 ❑ NFPA 13R ❑ NFPA 13D

Standpipes: ❑ No ❑ Yes Class ❑ I ❑ II ❑ III ❑ Wet ❑ Dry

Fire District: ❑ No ❑ Yes (Primary) Flood Hazard Area: ❑ No ❑ Yes

Building Height: (feet)_____

Gross Building Area:

Floor	Existing (sq ft)	New (sq ft)	Subtotal
6th Floor			
5th Floor			
4th Floor			
3rd Floor			
2nd Floor			
Mezzanine			
1st Floor			
Basement			

TOTAL

ALLOWABLE AREA

Occupancy:

Assembly	❏ A-1 ❏ A-2 ❏ A-3 ❏ A-4 ❏ A-5
Business	❏
Educational	❏
Factory	❏ F-1 Moderate ❏ F-2 Low
Hazardous	❏ H-1 Detonate ❏ H-2 Deflagrate ❏ H-3 Combust ❏ H-4 Health ❏ H-5 HPM
Institutional	❏ I-1 ❏ I-2 ❏ I-3 ❏ I-4
I-3 Condition	❏ 1 ❏ 2 ❏ 3 ❏ 4 ❏ 5
Mercantile	❏
Residential	❏ R-1 ❏ R-2 ❏ R-3 ❏ R-4
Storage	❏ S-1 Moderate ❏ S-2 Low ❏ High-piled
	❏ Parking Garage ❏ Open ❏ Enclosed ❏ Repair Garage
Utility and Miscellaneous	❏

Accessory Occupancies:

Assembly	❏ A-1 ❏ A-2 ❏ A-3 ❏ A-4 ❏ A-5
Business	❏
Educational	❏
Factory	❏ F-1 Moderate ❏ F-2 Low
Hazardous	❏ H-1 Detonate ❏ H-2 Deflagrate ❏ H-3 Combust ❏ H-4 Health ❏ H-5 HPM
Institutional	❏ I-1 ❏ I-2 ❏ I-3 ❏ I-4
I-3 Condition	❏ 1 ❏ 2 ❏ 3 ❏ 4 ❏ 5
Mercantile	❏
Residential	❏ R-1 ❏ R-2 ❏ R-3 ❏ R-4
Storage	❏ S-1 Moderate ❏ S-2 Low ❏ High-piled
	❏ Parking Garage ❏ Open ❏ Enclosed ❏ Repair Garage
Utility and Miscellaneous	❏

Accessory Occupancies:

❏ Furnace room where any piece of equipment is over 400,000 Btu per hour input

❏ Rooms with boilers where the largest piece of equipment is over 15 psi and 10 horsepower

❏ Refrigerant machine room

❏ Hydrogen cutoff rooms, not classified as Group H

❏ Incinerator rooms

❏ Paint shops, not classified as Group H, located in occupancies other than Group F

❏ Laboratories and vocational shops, not classified as Group H. located in a Group E or I-2 occupancy

❏ Laundry rooms over 100 square feet

❏ Group I-3 cells equipped with padded surfaces

❏ Group I-2 waste and linen collection rooms

❏ Waste and linen collection rooms over 100 square feet

❏ Stationary storage battery systems having a liquid electrolyte capacity of more than 50 gallons, or a lithium-ion capacity of 1,000 pounds used for facility standby power, emergency power or uninterrupted power supplies

❏ Rooms containing fire pumps

❏ Group I-2 storage rooms over 100 square feet

❏ Group I-2 commercial kitchens

❏ Group I-2 laundries equal to or less than 100 square feet

❏ Group I-2 rooms or spaces that contain fuel-fired heating equipment

Special Uses: ❏ 402 ❏ 403 ❏ 404 ❏ 405 ❏ 406 ❏ 407 o 408 ❏ 409 ❏ 410 ❏ 411 ❏ 412 ❏ 413 ❏ 414 ❏ 415 ❏ 416 ❏ 417 ❏ 418 ❏ 419 ❏ 420 ❏ 421 ❏ 422 o 423 ❏ 424 ❏ 425 ❏ 426 ❏ 427

Special Provisions: ❏ 509.2 ❏ 509.3 ❏ 509.4 ❏ 509.5 ❏ 509.6 ❏ 509.7 ❏ 509.8 ❏ 509.9

continued

ALLOWABLE AREA—cont'd

Mixed Occupancy: ❏ No ❏ Yes Separation: _____ Hr. Exception: _____

❏ Incidental Use Separation (508.2.5)
This separation is not exempt as a Nonseparated Use (see exceptions).

❏ Nonseparated Use (508.3.2)
The required type of construction for the building shall be determined by applying the height and area limitations for each of the applicable occupancies to the entire building. The most restrictive type of construction, so determined, shall apply to the entire building.

❏ Separated Use (508.3.3) - See below for area calculations
For each story, the area of the occupancy shall be such that the sum of the ratios of the actual floor area of each use divided by the allowable floor area for each use shall not exceed 1.

$$\frac{Actual\ Area\ of\ Occupancy\ A}{Allowable\ Area\ of\ Occupancy\ A} + \frac{Actual\ Area\ of\ Occupancy\ B}{Allowable\ Area\ of\ Occupancy\ B} \leq 1$$

_____ + _____ + ... = _____ ≤ 1.00

STORY NO.	DESCRIPTION AND USE	(A) BLDG AREA PER STORY (ACTUAL)	(B) TABLE 503[5] AREA	(C) AREA FOR FRONTAGE INCREASE[1]	(D) AREA FOR SPRINKLER INCREASE[2]	(E) ALLOWABLE AREA OR UNLIMITED[3]	(F) MAXIMUM BUILDING AREA[4]

1. Frontage area increases from Section 506.2 are computed thus:
   a. Perimeter which fronts a public way or open space having 20 feet minimum width = _____ (F)
   b. Total Building Perimeter = _____ (P)
   c. Ratio (F/P) = _____ (F/P)
   d. W = Minimum width of public way = _____ (W)
   e. Percent of frontage increase $I_f = 100\ [\ F/P - 0.25] \times W/30 =$ _____ (%)
2. The sprinkler increase per Section 506.3 is as follows:
   a. Multi-story building I_s = 200 percent
   b. Single story building I_s = 300 percent
3. Unlimited area applicable under conditions of Section 507.
4. Maximum Building Area = total number of stories in the building × E (506.4).
5. The maximum area of open parking garages must comply with Table 406.3.5. The maximum area of air traffic control towers must comply with Table 412.1.2.

ALLOWABLE HEIGHT

	ALLOWABLE (TABLE 503)	INCREASE FOR SPRINKLERS	SHOWN ON PLANS	CODE REFERENCE
Type of Construction	Type _____		Type _____	
Building Height in Feet		Feet = H + 20' = _____		
Building Height in Stories		Stories + 1 = _____		

FIRE PROTECTION REQUIREMENTS

BUILDING ELEMENT	FIRE SEPARATION DISTANCE (FEET)	RATING		DETAIL # AND SHEET #	DESIGN # FOR RATED ASSEMBLY	DESIGN # FOR RATED PENETRATION	DESIGN # FOR RATED JOINTS
		REQ'D	PROVIDED (W/ _____* REDUCTION)				
Structural Frame Including columns, girders, trusses							
Bearing Walls							
Exterior							
North							
East							
West							
South							
Interior							
Nonbearing walls and partitions Exterior walls							
North							
East							
West							
South							
Interior walls and partitions							
Floor Construction Including supporting beams and joists							
Roof Construction Including supporting beams and joists							
Shaft Enclosures — Exit							
Shaft Enclosures — Other							
Corridor Separation							
Occupancy Separation							
Party/Fire Wall Separation							
Smoke Barrier Separation							
Tenant Separation							
Incidental Use Separation							

* Indicate section number permitting reduction

LIFE SAFETY SYSTEM REQUIREMENTS

Emergency Lighting:	❏ No	❏ Yes	
Exit Signs:	❏ No	❏ Yes	
Fire Alarm:	❏ No	❏ Yes	
Smoke Detection Systems:	❏ No	❏ Yes	❏ Partial _____
Panic Hardware:	❏ No	❏ Yes	

LIFE SAFETY PLAN REQUIREMENTS

Life Safety Plan Sheet #: _____

❏ Fire and/or smoke rated wall locations (Chapter 7)
❏ Assumed and real property line locations
❏ Exterior wall opening area with respect to distance to assumed property lines (705.8)
❏ Existing structures within 30 feet of the proposed building
❏ Occupancy types for each area as it relates to occupant load calculation (Table 1004.1.1)
❏ Occupant loads for each area
❏ Exit access travel distances (1016)
❏ Common path of travel distances (1014.3 & 1028.8)
❏ Dead end lengths (1018.4)
❏ Clear exit widths for each exit door
❏ Maximum calculated occupant load capacity each exit door can accommodate based on egress width (1005.1)
❏ Actual occupant load for each exit door
❏ A separate schematic plan indicating where fire rated floor/ceiling and/or roof structure is provided for purposes of occupancy separation
❏ Location of doors with panic hardware (1008.1.10)
❏ Location of doors with delayed egress locks and the amount of delay (1008.1.9.7)
❏ Location of doors with electromagnetic egress locks (1008.1.9.8)
❏ Location of doors equipped with hold-open devices
❏ Location of emergency escape windows (1029)
❏ The square footage of each fire area (902)
❏ The square footage of each smoke compartment (407.4)
❏ Note any code exceptions or table notes that may have been utilized regarding the items above

ACCESSIBLE DWELLING UNITS
(SECTION 1107)

TOTAL UNITS	ACCESSIBLE UNITS REQUIRED	ACCESSIBLE UNITS PROVIDED	TYPE A UNITS REQUIRED	TYPE A UNITS PROVIDED	TYPE B UNITS REQUIRED	TYPE B UNITS PROVIDED	TOTAL ACCESSIBLE UNITS PROVIDED

ACCESSIBILITY PARKING
(SECTION 1106)

LOT OR PARKING AREA	TOTAL # OF PARKING SPACES		# OF ACCESSIBLE SPACES PROVIDED			TOTAL # ACCESSIBLE PROVIDED
	REQUIRED	PROVIDED	REGULAR WITH 5' ACCESS AISLE	VAN SPACES WITH		
				132" ACCESS AISLE	8' ACCESS AISLE	
TOTAL						

STRUCTURAL DESIGN

DESIGN LOADS:

Importance Factors: Wind (I_W) _____

Snow (I_S) _____

Seismic (I_E) _____

Live Loads: Roof _____ psf

Mezzanine _____ psf

Floor _____ psf

Ground Snow Load: _____ psf

Wind Load: Basic Wind Speed _____ mph (ASCE-7)

Exposure Category _____

Wind Base Shears (for MWFRS) V_x = _____ V_y = _____

SEISMIC DESIGN CATEGORY: ❑ A ❑ B ❑ C ❑ D

Provide the following Seismic Design Parameters:

Occupancy Category (Table 1604.5)   ❑ I ❑ II ❑ III ❑ IV

Spectral Response Acceleration S_S _____ %g S_1 _____ %g

Site Classification (Table 1613.5.2)   ❑ A ❑ B ❑ C ❑ D ❑ E ❑ F

Data Source: ❑ Field Test ❑ Presumptive ❑ Historical Data

Basic structural system (check one)

❑ Bearing Wall   ❑ Dual w/Special Moment Frame

❑ Building Frame   ❑ Dual w/Intermediate R/C or Special Steel

❑ Moment Frame   ❑ Inverted Pendulum

Seismic base shear: V_x = _____ V_y = _____

Analysis Procedure: ❑ Simplified ❑ Equivalent Lateral Force ❑ Dynamic

Architectural, Mechanical, Components anchored? ❑ Yes ❑ No

LATERAL DESIGN CONTROL: ❑ Earthquake   ❑ Wind

SOIL BEARING CAPACITIES:

Field Test (provide copy of test report) _____ psf

Presumptive Bearing capacity _____ psf

Pile size, type, and capacity _____

SPECIAL INSPECTIONS REQUIRED: ❑ Yes ❑ No

PLUMBING FIXTURE REQUIREMENTS
(TABLE 2902.1)

USE		WATERCLOSETS		URINALS	LAVATORIES		SHOWERS/ TUBS	DRINKING FOUNTAINS	
		MALE	FEMALE		MALE	FEMALE		REGULAR	ACCESSIBLE
SPACE	EXISTING								
	NEW								
	REQUIRED								

SPECIAL APPROVALS

Special approval: (Local Jurisdiction, Department of Insurance, OSC, DPI, DHHS, ICC, etc., describe below)

_____

_____

_____

ENERGY SUMMARY

ENERGY REQUIREMENTS:

The following data shall be considered minimum and any special attribute required to meet the energy code shall also be provided. Each Designer shall furnish the required portions of the project information for the plan data sheet. If performance method, state the annual energy cost for the standard reference design versus the annual energy cost for the proposed design.

Climate Zone: ❏ 3 ❏ 4 ❏ 5

Method of Compliance:
      ❏ Prescriptive (Energy Code)
      ❏ Performance (Energy Code)
      ❏ Prescriptive (ASHRAE 90.1)
      ❏ Performance (ASHRAE 90.1)

THERMAL ENVELOPE

Roof/ceiling Assembly (each assembly)
    Description of assembly: _____
    U-Value of total assembly: _____
    R-Value of insulation: _____
    Skylights in each assembly: _____
        U-Value of skylight: _____
    total square footage of skylights in each assembly: _____

Exterior Walls (each assembly)
    Description of assembly: _____
    U-Value of total assembly: _____
    R-Value of insulation: _____
    Openings (windows or doors with glazing)
        U-Value of assembly: _____
        Solar heat gain coefficient: _____
        projection factor: _____
        Door R-Values: _____

Walls below grade (each assembly)
    Description of assembly: _____
    U-Value of total assembly: _____
    R-Value of insulation: _____

Floors over unconditioned space (each assembly)
    Description of assembly: _____
    U-Value of total assembly: _____
    R-Value of insulation: _____

Floors slab on grade
    Description of assembly: _____
    U-Value of total assembly: _____
    R-Value of insulation: _____
    Horizontal/vertical requirement: _____
    slab heated: _____

MECHANICAL SUMMARY

MECHANICAL SYSTEMS, SERVICE SYSTEMS AND EQUIPMENT

Thermal Zone

winter dry bulb: _____

summer dry bulb: _____

Interior design conditions

winter dry bulb: _____

summer dry bulb: _____

relative humidity: _____

Building heating load: _____

Building cooling load: _____

Mechanical Spacing Conditioning System

Unitary

description of unit: _____

heating efficiency: _____

cooling efficiency: _____

size category of unit: _____

Boiler

Size category. If oversized, state reason.: _____

Chiller

Size category. If oversized, state reason.: _____

List equipment efficiencies: _____

ELECTRICAL SUMMARY

ELECTRICAL SYSTEM AND EQUIPMENT

Method of Compliance:

Energy Code: ❏ Prescriptive ❏ Performance

ASHRAE 90.1: ❏ Prescriptive ❏ Performance

Lighting schedule (each fixture type)

lamp type required in fixture

number of lamps in fixture

ballast type used in the fixture

number of ballasts in fixture

total wattage per fixture

total interior wattage specified vs. allowed (whole building or space by space)

total exterior wattage specified vs. allowed

Additional Prescriptive Compliance

❏ 506.2.1 More Efficient Mechanical Equipment

❏ 506.2.2 Reduced Lighting Power Density

❏ 506.2.3 Energy Recovery Ventilation Systems

❏ 506.2.4 Higher Efficiency Service Water Heating

❏ 506.2.5 On-site Supply of Renewable Energy

❏ 506.2.6 Automatic Daylighting Control Systems

APPENDIX C
CODE CHANGE PROPOSAL
NORTH CAROLINA
BUILDING CODE COUNCIL

322 Chapanoke Road, Suite 200
Raleigh, North Carolina 27603
(919) 661-5880
Petition for Rule Making

Item Number_____

Granted by BCC _____Adopted by BCC _____Approved by RRC _____

Denied by BCC _____Disapproved by BCC_____Objection by RRC _____

PROPONENT_____ PHONE (___)___ -_____.
REPRESENTING_____ _____
ADDRESS _____
CITY_____ STATE _____ ZIP _____
E-MAIL _____ FAX (___)___ -_____.

North Carolina State Building Code, Volume_____   Section_____

CHECK ONE: [ ] Revise section to read as follows: [ ] Delete section and substitute the following.
                      [ ] Add new section to read as follows: [ ] Delete section without substitution.

~~LINE THROUGH MATERIAL TO BE DELETED~~   <u>UNDERLINE MATERIAL TO BE ADDED</u>

Type or print. Continue proposal or reason on plain paper attached to this form. See reverse side for instructions.

Will this proposal add to the cost of construction? Yes [ ]   No [ ]
Explain total economic impact for added cost or savings in REASON.
Provide a fiscal analysis of any increase (or decrease) in cost.

REASON:

BCC CODE CHANGES

Signature_____   DATE:_____   FORM 1/1/12

INSTRUCTIONS

Each proposed code change request shall comply with the following rules:

Rule 1: Twenty-one (21) copies of the proposed Petiton for Rule-making along with supporting documentation shall be filed with the Building Code Council Secretary.

Rule 2: The filing shall be received by the first day of the month prior to the quarterly scheduled meeting date.

Rule 3: Each request shall be legibly printed, typewritten, or copied on this form and shall contain the following:

(1) The proposed rule change must be set forth in full and contain explicit reference to the affected section or sections of the code.

(2) The request shall state the reasons for the proposed rule change with supporting documentation.

(3) The proposed rule change shall comply with the standards set forth in GS 143-138(c) and reference to the particular standards shall be set forth in the request for the amendment.

(4) The proposed rule change shall contain an economic impact analysis as required by GS 143-138(a).

Rule 4: When a request is improperly filed or not in accordance with all the rules listed above, the Council Secretary shall reject the submittal and notify the applicant of the proper procedure to follow.

Rule 5: Upon the proper filing of a request, the Council Secretary shall forward one copy of said request to each council member prior to the scheduled meeting date. Persons filing proposed petitions are hereby notified of the place and time of the scheduled hearings. The Council Secretary shall cause to be published the notice of public hearing as specified in GS 143-138(a).

Rule 6: The Council shall either grant or deny the proposed Petition for Rule-making at the meeting following receipt of the proposed rule change. The Council will take no further action on items that are Denied. Granted items may be referred to Committee for review.

Rule 7: The Council will hold a public hearing on granted items at the next quarterly scheduled meeting. The Council will take final action on granted items at the next quarterly scheduled meeting after the public hearing.

Timeline Example	
Petetion Received:	February 1
Petition Granted:	March BCC meeting
Notice of Hearing Published:	April NC Register
Committee Review:	April - May
Hearing Held:	June BCC meeting
Final Adoption:	September BCC meeting
Rules Review Hearing:	November RRC meeting
Approved:	December 1

APPENDIX D

AFFIDAVIT OF WORKERS' COMPENSATION COVERAGE
N.C.G.S. §87-14

The undersigned applicant for Building Permit # _____ being the

_____ Contractor

_____ Owner

_____ Officer/Agent of the Contractor or Owner

Do hereby aver under penalties of perjury that the person(s), firm(s) or corporation(s) performing the work set forth in the permit:

_____ has/have three (3) or more employees and have obtained workers' compensation insurance to cover them,

_____ has/have one or more subcontractor(s) and have obtained workers' compensation insurance to cover them,

_____ has/have one or more subcontractor(s) who has/have their own policy of workers' compensation covering themselves,

_____ has/have not more than two (2) employees and no subcontractors,

while working on the project for which this permit is sought. It is understood that the Inspection Department issuing the permit may require certificates of coverage of workers, compensation insurance prior to issuance of the permit and at any time during the permitted work from any person, firm or corporation carrying out the work.

Firm name: _____

By: _____

Title: _____

Date: _____

APPENDIX E
APPEALS
NORTH CAROLINA
BUILDING CODE COUNCIL

322 Chapanoke Road, Suite 200
Raleigh, North Carolina 27603
(919) 661-5880

APPEAL TO NCDOI/NCBCC   Hearing Date_____/_____/_____

GS 153A-374, GS 160A-434	GS 143-140, GS 143-141
Formal Interpretation by NCDOI_____	Appeal of Local Decision to NCBCC_____
Appeal of Local Decision to NCDOI_____	Appeal of NCDOI Decision to NCBCC_____

APPELLANT_____ PHONE (___)___ -_____ X _____.
REPRESENTING_____
ADDRESS _____
CITY_____ STATE _____ ZIP _____
E-MAIL _____ FAX (____)_____ -_____.

North Carolina State Building Code, Volume _____ - Section_____

REQUEST ONE: [ ] Formal Interpretation by NCDOI   [ ] Appeal of Local Decision to NCBCC
                    [ ] Appeal of Local Decision to NCDOI   [ ] Appeal of NCDOI Decision to NCBCC

Type or print. Include all background information as required by the referenced General Statutes and the attached policies. Attach additional supporting information.

REASON:

APPEAL TO NCDOI/NCBCC

Signature_____   DATE:_____   FORM 1/1/12

202.9 Appeals.

202.9.1 Engineering Division. A written technical interpretation shall be provided as specified in Section 203.1.2.1.2. Any person may appeal in writing an order, decision, or determination pertaining to the code or any state building law by filing written notice with the Commissioner of Insurance or his designee within 10 days after the order, decision or determination. A copy of the appeal shall be furnished to each party.

(General Statutes 143-140, 153A-374 and 160A-434)

203.1.2.1 Interpretations.

203.1.2.1.1 Informal interpretations. The Engineering Division shall provide informal interpretations on code related matters either by e-mail, letter or telephone. These informal interpretations may be accepted by the local code enforcement official or party requesting the interpretation. Either party may request a formal interpretation of the code.

203.1.2.1.2 Formal interpretations. Any person may request in writing a formal interpretation of the code. The request shall be addressed to the Chief Code Consultant for the Department of Insurance. The request shall be specific and shall reference the code sections in question. All formal interpretations shall be in writing. A formal interpretation shall be binding on all parties unless appealed to the Building Code Council as specified in Section 201.9.2. Formal interpretations determined to be of a general nature may be posted on the department web site. (General Statute 143-140)

203.1.2.2 Appeals. Any person may appeal in writing an order, decision or determination of a code enforcement official pertaining to the code or any state building law. The appeal shall be addressed to the Chief Engineer for the Department of Insurance by filing written notice within 10 days after the order, decision or determination. The appeal shall contain the type and size of the building in question, the location of the building, and shall reference the code sections in question. The decision shall be in writing and shall set forth the facts found. The decision rendered shall be based on the technical provisions of the code, public health and safety and shall be construed liberally to those ends. A decision shall be binding on all parties unless an appeal is submitted to the Building Code Council as specified in Section 201.9.2. A copy of the appeal and written decision shall be furnished to each party.

(General Statutes 153A-374 and 160A-434)

202.9.2 Building Code Council. The Building Code Council shall hear appeals from the decisions of a state enforcement agencies relating to any matter related to the code. Any person wishing to appeal a decision of a state enforcement agency to the Building Code Council shall give written notice of appeal as follows:

202.9.2.1 Twenty-one copies including an original of the Notice of Appeal shall be filed with the Building Code Council c/o NC Department of Insurance, Engineering Division, 322 Chapanoke Road, Suite 200, Raleigh, NC 27603 and one copy shall be filed with the State enforcement agency from which the appeal is taken.

202.9.2.2 The Notice of Appeal shall be received no later than 30 days from the date of the decision of the State enforcement agency.

202.9.2.3 The Notice of Appeal shall be legibly printed, typewritten or copied and shall contain the following:

(1) Name, address of the party or parties requesting the appeal.

(2) The name of the State enforcement agency, the date of the decision from which the appeal is taken, and a copy of the written decision received from the enforcement agency.

(3) The decision from which the appeal is taken shall be set forth in full in the Notice of Appeal or a copy of the decision shall be attached to all copies of the Notice of Appeal.

(4) The contentions and allegations of fact must be set forth in full in a clear and concise manner with reference to the sections of the code in controversy.

(5) The original Notice of Appeal shall be signed by the party or parties filing appeal.

(6) The Notice of Appeal shall be received by the first day of the month prior to the Building Code Council's quarterly scheduled meeting in order to be placed on the agenda for that meeting. The Chairman may schedule a special meeting to hear an appeal.

202.9.2.4 Upon the proper filing of the Notice of Appeal, the Building Code Council Secretary shall forward one copy of the Notice of Appeal to each member of the Building Code Council. The Chairman may appoint a Hearing Committee to hear appeals. The Secretary shall send notice in writing to the party or parties requesting an appeal and to the Building Code Council Hearing Committee members at least 15 days prior to the Hearing Committee meeting. A written decision of the Hearing Committee meeting shall be provided to all Building Code Council Members. The actions of the Hearing Committee shall be final, unless appealed to the full Building Code Council in writing within 30 days of the Hearing Committee's action. If a Hearing Committee consists of at least seven council members, it will constitute a quorum of the full council. Further appeals shall be as specified in Section 202.9.3.

202.9.2.5 The Building Code Council shall, upon a motion of the State enforcement agency or on its own motion, dismiss appeals for the following reasons:

1. Not pursued by the appellant or withdrawn;

2. Appeal not filed in accordance with these rules; or

3. Lack of jurisdiction.

202.9.2.6 When the Building Code Council finds that a State enforcement agency was in error in its interpretation of the code, the Building Code Council shall remand the case to the agency with instructions to take such actions as the Building Code Council directs. When the Building Code Council finds on appeal that materials or methods of construction proposed are equivalent to those required by the code, the Building Code Council shall remand the case to the State enforcement agency with instructions to permit the use of such materials or methods of construction. The Building Code Council shall immediately initiate procedures for amending the code to permit the use of such materials or methods of construction.

202.9.2.7 The Building Code Council shall provide a written decision setting forth the findings of fact and the Building Code Council's conclusions to each party or parties filing the appeal and to the state enforcement agency from which the appeal was taken.

202.9.3 Superior court. Whenever any person desires to appeal a decision of the Building Code Council or a decision of a State or local enforcement agency, he may appeal either to the Wake County Superior Court or the Superior Court of the county in which the proposed building is to be situated in accordance with the provisions of Chapter 150B of the General Statutes.

[General Statute 143-141(d)]

APPENDIX F

STATE OF NORTH CAROLINA

OWNER EXEMPTION AFFIDAVIT
PURSUANT TO G.S. 87-14(a)(1)

COUNTY OF _____

_____ Inspections Department

Address and Parcel Identification of Real Property Where Building is to be Constructed or Altered:
_____.

I, _____,

(Print Full Name)

hereby claim an exemption from licensure under G.S. 87-1(b)(2) by initialing the relevant provision in paragraph 1 and initialing paragraphs 2-4 below and attesting to the following:

1. _____ I certify that I am the owner of the property set forth above on which this building is to be constructed or altered;

OR

_____ I am legally authorized to act on behalf of the firm or corporation which is constructing or altering this building on the property owned by the firm or corporation as set forth above (name of firm or corporation: _____);

2. _____ I will personally superintend and manage all aspects of the construction or alternation of the building and that duty will not be delegated to any person not duly licensed under the terms of Article 1 of Chapter 87 of the General Statutes of North Carolina;

3. _____ I will be personally present for all inspections required by the North Carolina State Building Code, unless the plans for the construction or alteration of the building were drawn and sealed by an architect licensed pursuant to Chapter 83A of the General Statutes of North Carolina;

4. _____ I understand that a copy of this AFFIDAVIT will be transmitted to the North Carolina Licensing Board for General Contractors for verification that I am validly entitled to claim an exemption under G.S. 87-1(b)(2) for the building construction or alteration specified herein. I further understand that, if the North Carolina Licensing Board for General Contractors determines that I was not entitled to claim this exemption, the building permit issued for the building construction or alteration specified herein shall be revoked pursuant to G.S. 153A-362 or G.S. 160A-422.

_____   _____

(Signature of Affiant)   Date

Sworn to (or affirmed) and Subscribed before me this the ____ day of _____, 20_____

_____

Signature of Notary Public

_____

Printed Name of Notary Public

My Commission Expires:_____(Notary Stamp or Seal)

(NOTE: It is a Class F felony to willfully commit perjury in any affidavit taken pursuant to law—G.S. 14-209)

To: All NC Building Code Enforcement Jurisdictions

The North Carolina Licensing Board for General Contractors is currently implementing procedures to comply with recently enacted changes to NC General Statute 87-14. Effective June 27, 2011 for projects costing $30,000 or more, property owners claiming exemption to the general contractor licensing requirement when applying for a building permit are required, before being entitled to the permit, to execute a verified affidavit attesting:

a. That the person is the owner of the property on which the building is being constructed or, in the case of a firm or corporation, is legally authorized to act on behalf of the firm or corporation.

b. That the person will personally superintend and manage all aspects of the construction of the building and that the duty will not be delegated to any other person not duly licensed.

c. That the person will be personally present for all inspections required by the North Carolina State Building Code, unless the plans for the building were drawn and sealed by an architect licensed pursuant to Chapter 83A of the General Statutes.

The statute further requires that a copy of the affidavit be transmitted to the North Carolina Licensing Board for General Contractors for the purpose of verifying the applicant was validly entitled to claim the exemption. If during the permitting process any irregularities are detected that call in to question whether a permit applicant is fully complying with all applicable laws, the person issuing the permit should make note of the circumstances when forwarding information to the Board and provide a copy of the building permit application, including contact information for any subcontractors listed. **Please be aware the new requirements are not intended to delay the issuance of the building permit. When the person applying for the building permit reasonably satisfies the permitting authority that the applicable laws are being complied with, and executes all required documents, the building permit should be issued without delay.** Upon review of the documents, should any irregularities be detected that require further action, the Board's staff will contact the code enforcement authority.

Whenever possible, the most practical method of submitting affidavits to the Board is to scan the documents and transmit them as PDF email attachments to the appropriate Field Investigator serving the various code enforcement jurisdictions throughout the state. Specific email addresses have been set up for this purpose. Alternately, the documents may be faxed or sent via US Mail. Attached to this email are pages with the assigned territories, email addresses for affidavit transmittal, fax numbers and contact information for the Board's field staff. Please contact the staff member serving your area with any questions you may have. Also attached to this email is a model affidavit developed by the NC Home Builders Association in conjunction with the UNC School of Government. You may use this model affidavit or develop your own, as long as all the required information is provided. Additional information is available on the UNC School of Government website using the following link: http://www.sog.unc.edu/node/767.

Thank you for your assistance in this matter. The Board sincerely appreciates your cooperation in implementing these new requirements.

Field Investigator Districts

Mike Silver (Western) 828-688-3803, Fax: 828-688-2011
Affidavit Email: mikesilver@nclbgc.org

Alexander	Buncombe	Cherokee	Haywood	Madison	Rutherford	Wilkes
Alleghany	Burke	Clay	Henderson	McDowell	Swain	Yadkin
Ashe	Caldwell	Cleveland	Jackson	Mitchell	Transylvania	Yancey
Avery	Catawba	Graham	Macon	Polk	Watauga	

Curtis Huff (Upper Piedmont) 919-690-8734, Fax: 919-690-8739
Affidavit Email: curtishuff@nclbgc.org

Alamance	Forsyth	Nash	Stokes
Caswell	Guilford	Orange	Surry
Chatham	Halifax	Person	Wake
Durham	Harnett	Rockingham	Warren

Kenny McCombs (Lower Piedmont) 704-933-5554, Fax: 704-933-5554
Affidavit Email: kennymccombs@nclbgc.org

Anson	Gaston	Montgomery	Union
Cabarrus	Iredell	Randolph	
Davie	Lincoln	Rowan	
Davidson	Mecklenburg	Stanly	

Mike Brown (Coastal-North Eastern) 252-758-3040, Fax: 252-758-3080
Affidavit Email: mikebrown@nclbgc.org

Beaufort	Currituck	Gates	Hyde	Pamlico	Tyrell	Wilson
Bertie	Dare	Granville	Lenoir	Pasquotank	Vance	
Camden	Edgecombe	Greene	Martin	Perquimans	Washington	
Chowan	Franklin	Hertford	Northampton	Pitt	Wayne	

Joel A. Macon (Coastal-South Eastern) 910-458-8899, Fax: 910-458-8899
Affidavit Email: joelmacon@nclbgc.org

Bladen	Craven	Johnston	New Hanover	Robeson
Brunswick	Cumberland	Jones	Onslow	Sampson
Carteret	Duplin	Lee	Pender	Scotland
Columbus	Hoke	Moore	Richmond	

Affidavits transmitted to the Board via US Mail should be sent to:

Susan Sullivan
NC Licensing Board for General Contractors
P.O. Box 17187
Raleigh, North Carolina 27619